THE
LIVING ROOM
DESIGN
FORMULA

THE **LIVING ROOM** DESIGN FORMULA

*Style Your Home like a Pro,
One Room at a Time*

by

AMY LEAH BARRICKMAN

The Living Room Design Formula © Copyright 2025 Amy Leah Barrickman

All rights reserved. No part of this publication may be reproduced, distributed, or transmitted in any form or by any means, including photocopying, recording, or other electronic or mechanical methods, without the prior written permission of the publisher, except in the case of brief quotations embodied in critical reviews and certain other noncommercial uses permitted by copyright law.

Although the author and publisher have made every effort to ensure that the information in this book was correct at press time, the author and publisher do not assume and hereby disclaim any liability to any party for any loss, damage, or disruption caused by errors or omissions, whether such errors or omissions result from negligence, accident, or any other cause.

Adherence to all applicable laws and regulations, including international, federal, state, and local governing professional licensing, business practices, advertising, and all other aspects of doing business in the US, Canada, or any other jurisdiction is the sole responsibility of the reader and consumer.

Neither the author nor the publisher assumes any responsibility or liability whatsoever on behalf of the consumer or reader of this material. Any perceived slight of any individual or organization is purely unintentional.

Neither the author nor the publisher can be held responsible for the use of the information provided within this book.

For more information, email Info@BarrickmanDesign.com

ISBN: 979-8-89694-022-7 - eBook

ISBN: 979-8-89694-023-4 - Paperback

ISBN: 979-8-89694-024-1 - Hardcover

GET YOUR COMPLIMENTARY GIFTS

Implement the ideas in this book faster with the resources available for instant download at www.BarrickmanDesign.com

Living Room Measurement and Layout Guide

Helpful tools to help you plan your space, including graph paper, sample layouts, and to-scale furniture footprints to play around with in your room design.

Gallery Wall Tips & Tricks

A step-by-step guide to creating a beautiful feature in your home using photographs.

FOLLOW ME
@BARRICKMANDESIGN
FOR REGULAR DESIGN TIPS AND UPDATES!

For Jenny, who wandered into a fabric store and became part of the fabric of my life. You have given me a career, a second family, and countless hours of fun!

TABLE OF CONTENTS

Introduction: What Matters More than Your Home? 1
Chapter 1: How to Use This Book 3
    Other People's Opinions 4
    You're Hosting 5
    Take Action 7
Chapter 2: Determine Your Wants and Needs 9
    Imagine All the Possibilities 9
    Analyze Your Use of the Room 14
    Special Use Cases 16
Chapter 3: Mapping Your Space 19
    Measure and Draw Your Space 20
    Determine Your Layout 22
    Create a Nook 26
    Built-in Bookcases 27
    Other Storage Ideas 31
    Add Accent Furniture 32
Chapter 4: Lighting and Electrical Plan 34
    Lighting Plan 35
    Overhead Lighting 36
    Decorative Lighting 38
    Accent Lighting 40
    Ceiling Fans 41
    Switches 41
    Dimmers 42
    Lightbulbs 43
    Other Electrical Elements 45

Chapter 5: Creating Your Mood Board 53
Finding Inspiration 54
Choose a Focal Point for Your Space 55
Develop Other Categories 56
Group Your Images 57
Make It Official 58
Add Interest and Texture 58

Chapter 6: Primary Seating 61
Budget 63
Browse for Your Primary Seating 65
Pillow Selection 70
Confirm Measurements and Order 72

Chapter 7: Center Table Selection 74
Size 74
Material 76

Chapter 8: Light Fixture Selection 79
Lighting Size 81
Placement 82
Lighting Needs 83
Style 83

Chapter 9: Rugs 91
Rug Size 92
Carpet Composition and Weave 94

Chapter 10: Walls 99
Types of Wallpaper 100
Wall Paint 103

Chapter 11: Accent Furniture 108
Side Tables 108
Console Tables 110
Accent Chairs and Ottomans 110

Chapter 12: Window Treatments 112
Roman Shades 112
Drapes 116
Choosing Fabric for Drapes or Roman Shades 120

Privacy and Light Filtering *122*
Hardware *123*

Chapter 13: Wall Art 127
Choose Your Leading Wall *127*
Photography *128*
Art *130*

Chapter 14: Accessories 136
Objets d'Art *137*
Areas to Arrange *144*

Chapter 15: Installation 151

Introduction

What Matters More than Your Home?

Aside from the people in our lives, the place we live is arguably the most important to us. Your space is a reflection of you, and living in a room you love can change the way you feel.

Making your space look beautiful isn't easy. There is a reason the rich and famous hire expensive designers to outfit their spaces. It may seem out of reach for some, but *anyone* can create a space they're proud of.

As I developed my design practice over the last fifteen years, I realized that designing a living space follows a formula. In this book, I have broken down the formula into simple steps that anyone can follow to create a beautiful and functional room. We will create your dream room together, and I am honored to be part of the process as I walk you through each step and share some stories.

It does not matter if you're working on your formal living room or casual family room or anything in between, this book will give you the tools to call it finished.

I have to warn you, though, about the number one enemy of design: indecision. Do not wait; make the decision to get started on your room now. Creating your own room will take a little bit of persistence, but we will make it fun. You're going to love the way your space looks!

Thank you for choosing Barrickman Design—I can't wait to see what you create!

Amy Leah Barrickman

Chapter 1

How to Use This Book

Design projects can go on forever, but not this one. While a room is never truly finished, I will teach you how to tackle the space so you can actually call it done. Whether you love design or are completely overwhelmed by it, this book will give you the tools you need to create your own beautiful space. All I need from you is the commitment that you'll go through the steps and do it.

As mentioned, indecision is a common issue in design, and I understand why it is so hard for people to choose what to put in their space. It's human nature to think that if we continue to look at options, we will find clarity, but my experience shows that more options do not create a better outcome. In fact, the more choices you have, the more muddy your decisions become.

For that reason I will ask you to commit to various things through this process. First, carve out fifteen minutes each day to work on your room. You are allowed to spend more time, of course, but not any less. When you are consistent, your design ideas will come together easily.

Next, read this book in sequential order. In school the teacher goes through basic skills in the beginning of the year. Those early lessons might seem superfluous, but they are important because future material builds on them. This book is structured in the same way. Even if it seems as though you could skip a step, you will get the best results if you go through it from start to finish.

Last, when you feel stuck—it happens to professional designers too—do your best to go through each chapter and the best result will make itself clear. You can always go back and revisit a section, but please don't skip ahead.

I am so excited to walk you through this process, and I will be your cheerleader! You may find that not everyone in your life is, knowingly or unknowingly, as supportive though.

Other People's Opinions

I could design a room a hundred different ways and they'd all be beautiful and functional, but only *you* can decide which one you want to live in. Your friends and family probably wouldn't select the same design that you would, and that's okay because all the designs are great!

The people who love and care about you, perhaps the people who share this space with you, are going to have lots of opinions, and their opinions will only delay your results. Your loved ones' opinions matter, of course, but declare yourself captain of this ship. Consider their feedback the same way you'd consider a child's birthday wish list. You want to get them something they want and that makes them happy, but you also need to make the best decision from your point of view.

If you choose to share your plans with someone, do not ask for their input. I know it sounds rude, but I cannot emphasize it enough: Present your ideas as being firm. Be especially protective of the *star* of your room—which we will discuss later in this book. Some people (I'm looking at you, mothers-in-law) have a very powerful ability to throw designs off-kilter. I've seen clients fall into analysis paralysis and delay their finished product, or worse: end up with a watered-down version of the design they fell in love with.

We are embarking on a journey as a team. Sure, I can't physically be there with you, but I am your partner in this endeavor. This book is about designing a room without a designer, but really *I* am your designer. Know this, and if anyone gives you anything other than positive feedback, just pretend you're talking to me. Tell me what *you* really want. Sometimes you may see the design in a different light, and other times you may just shake off their ideas and come back to your truly lovely concept.

You're Hosting

We need a deadline, so you're having a party. Put a date on the calendar and plan to have someone over to see the space. It could be a big event or a friend for coffee, but choose a date and stick to it.

One of my clients hired me to help her design a formal living room in January, just after her famous annual holiday party. She asked how long the room would take to complete, and I joked, "We will have it complete before your party next year."

We both laughed because obviously a single room can be done in fewer than eleven months.

With no rush on the completion, we took time to look at furniture and place orders. It was coming together beautifully . . . until it wasn't. A discontinued fabric here, a damaged table there, suddenly it felt like we were swimming upstream.

What had once been a joke was now a very real deadline: the party was happening the first week of December, and this room needed to look amazing for it. I wanted other people to see the fabulous room, and more importantly I wanted my client to be satisfied.

There is nothing like a deadline to get you in gear! Instead of analyzing every available alternate option, I was laser focused on the things that would look the best and still arrive before the party.

The day of the party, I found myself at her house accepting a delivery and arranging last-minute accessories. Without the deadline, the project could have dragged on even longer.

I always ask my clients to throw a party so that I have a deadline. If the client doesn't want to, I tell them to lie to me. I need to believe the room must be completed by a certain date, and so do you.

Pencil in a date on the calendar, which you will confirm after the furniture selection.

Use these guidelines for choosing your date:

- *Rooms that include construction or custom cabinetry will take six–twelve months.*
- *Rooms that include custom furniture will take four to eight months.*

- Rooms that require electrical work will take two to three months.
- Rooms that will have custom window treatments made or wallpaper professionally installed will take two to three months.
- Rooms that are composed of ready-made furniture and decor will take one to three months.

Now that your party is penciled in, it's time to start dreaming! Start with broad ideas and methodically narrow them down in the next chapter.

> **Amy's Favorites**
>
> It is likely that you will feel stuck during at least one section of this book—even professionals get stalled in the process sometimes! Look for text boxes in each chapter providing Amy's Favorites with an easy suggestion that is a proven winner!

Take Action

At the end of each chapter, you will find a to-do list that summarizes the chapter's information and provides a guide to help you move forward. To get the most out of this book, make sure to complete the action steps.

Chapter 1 To-Do List

- Commit to completing your room.
- Spend fifteen minutes a day working on your room
- Read this book in sequential order
- Don't ask for advice
- Pick a potential date for your party

Chapter 2

Determine Your Wants and Needs

What is the difference between a picture from a catalog and a space created by a professional designer? *You*! Designers understand how to tailor a space to the people who live in it. Luckily for you, no one knows your space and the needs of the people who use it better than you do.

Imagine All the Possibilities

I begin each and every project the same way: by imagining all that is possible. No matter what the current space is like, consider all available options before committing to any aspect of a design. This is not the time to be limited by what already exists or your budget; this is the time to dream about all we could do to enhance your space and life.

Start by looking at your raw space, including the rooms that surround your living room. Even if your budget does not allow a major remodel in the near future, consider if you might alter the room or other spaces adjacent to it in the future.

I once worked with a client who wanted her dining room to be finished in time for Thanksgiving. As previously mentioned, I love deadlines. We put together a concept, and I couldn't wait to get back to the office to pull it all together. As I was walking out of the house, she breezily mentioned, "Someday we will do the kitchen—in the distant future." I thought nothing of it and got to work.

I was whirring with excitement when I presented the mood board. She loved the look. By the end of the day, I was ordering a gorgeous grass cloth to go on the walls, and by Thanksgiving, she was hosting in a room she loved.

Not even four months later she texted me that they were ready to do the kitchen. When I arrived for the kitchen discovery appointment, a feeling of dread came over me. "What if we need to take out this wall?" I thought, looking at a kitchen wall that was adjacent to the dining room and therefore covered by our gorgeous grass cloth on the opposite side. This wall treatment had been expensive, custom made and was, well, irreplaceable.

By the end of the appointment I realized that in order to give her the best design possible, we had to take out the majority of that wall and would also need to add a steel beam to support it. This meant that the grass cloth put up only a few months before would likely be damaged, either by construction or dust or both. Even if we were able to preserve the majority of it, ordering an additional roll at this point would be a futile effort. It had been custom dyed at production and a new run (at our expense, of course) was unlikely to match.

Had I known that the wall would potentially come out before designing the dining room, we could have done a number of things to avoid this situation. We could have held off on wallpaper completely or chosen one that was easier to match. At the very least I could have ordered a couple of extra rolls!

Designers are problem solvers, so I was able to come up with a solution that used millwork (wood treatment and molding) and paint to blend the spaces together. Ultimately, my client was happy with both spaces, but this experience was a big lesson for my design practice.

No matter what your budget is, make sure that every dollar you spend is leading you in the direction of your dream home. For this reason, make note of any opportunities you may take in the future. This space will last a very long time, or at least as long as home decor trends allow.

> **Note: If moving is in your near future**
>
> Even if you plan to sell your house in the near future, this exercise may uncover some simple changes that make your house more marketable.
>
> For example, one of the questions in the following exercise is about where you enter and exit the space. Many living rooms have several exterior doors in close proximity to one another. In this scenario I will ask the client to choose one door that will serve as the main thoroughfare. Usually, it's an easy choice because there is already one door that is used most frequently. With that decision made, you can make the other doors function as windows. If you choose to invest some

money and replace the superfluous exterior door, you may turn it into an arched window. That is the type of thing that makes a buyer fall in love with a house.

If you do not have the budget to replace the doors, you can convert the doors in appearance only by hanging drapes in a way that visually turns the door into a window. This is a beautiful and inexpensive upgrade that will enhance the space from a potential buyer's perspective.

Questions to Ask About Your Room

To capture the possibilities and understand your wants and needs, look around the space and think about which rooms are adjacent. Ask yourself the following questions and write down relevant answers and ideas:

- What would you do with the space if you had a magic wand?
- Which spaces are adjacent to your room? Do you like looking at them?
- What do you see when you look out the windows? Should you focus on the view or distract from it?
- Is there anything here that may change in the future?
- Is there a wall, or perhaps just a portion of a wall, that you could take down to create a better flow?
- Can you expand the room using space from an adjacent room?

- Are there spaces where you could add storage? (e.g., under an adjacent stairwell or with built-in units)
- Where do you enter and exit the room?
- Are there exterior doors and if so, which doors get the most use?
- Is there a better entry or exit point?
- Could you take out the ceiling and make it a vaulted space?
- Is there a doorway that could be widened?
- Is there a fireplace? Should there be?
- Could you incorporate an arch, beams, or other architectural detail?
- Does your space have areas that should be distinguished from one another? This is especially common in open-plan designs. If so, would adding a small wall help to delineate the space?

Review and Choose Priorities

Once you understand what's possible in the space, bring it down to project size. First, take a look at what ideas are most beneficial and which are most important to you. For example, a future kitchen renovation is important to most people, and if that's going to affect your living room, you need to consider the future kitchen in the decisions you make. Taking out a ceiling may not be important, but could be very beneficial. The removal of the ceiling may make other aspects of your design easier (e.g., electrical, insulation), and it is a huge visual payoff for a smaller percentage of the budget.

Analyze Your Use of the Room

You've considered what can be done; now think about how your space will best be used. One of my favorite parts of creating a space is tailoring it specifically for the people who live in it. For that reason, I want to know who uses the space, what time of day they use it, and how they use it. Think about how you use the room. Do you prefer to watch TV or read in the space? Would you like to host big family gatherings or just watch a movie with a companion there?

This is also your chance to consider what would make this room a ten out of ten. Do you wish you had a bar with cold seltzers at the ready? Would a sun-drenched reading chair give you a sense of contentment?

Room Use Exercise

The following exercise asks questions about room use and your preferences. Answer each question and make notes.

- Who uses the space the most?
- What activities do you use it for?
- What time of day do you most often use it?
- Who else uses the space occasionally?
- What is most functional about the space?
- What is least functional about the space?
- What do you enjoy looking at in this room?
- What would you prefer not to look at anymore?
- What do you love doing in this space?
- What do you wish that you could do in this space but cannot do currently?

- Are there any problems you'd like to solve with the design of this space?
- What would you be very happy to have, see, or do in this space?
- What would you like to store in this space?

Use your observations to solve problems in your space. For example, if your children often build forts in the space, note that you need a place to neatly store the blankets and pillows. If you regularly host parties in the space, note to search for flooring that is stain resistant and easy to clean. Use the design of the room to address any such issues.

I once worked with a client who had a regular live-in guest: her father-in-law. While she adored him, she did not adore his habit of trimming his toenails and leaving the remains on her coffee table. She told me this only for a laugh, but it made me realize we did not have a trash can in that room. While I do not usually put a trash can in a living room, I figured it wouldn't hurt to provide a receptacle for those pesky clippings.

Without saying a thing, I showed up the next time with a carefully selected trash can in a rattan weave that not only matched the decor but was also short enough to sit on the shelf under the coffee table. I walked in and said, "I have a gift for your father-in-law!" and tucked it under the table. She laughed and said I was "too much." During his next visit she pointed out how handy the little trash can was when she had a tissue to dispose of. As I am sure you can guess, the nail clippings found their way into the bin from then on.

Some of our design observations will be simple and our solutions may be small. It's easy to add a trash can after the design is complete, but it is not easy to rewire for a special sound system or build storage after a room is complete, so make notes now about what you can do to make this space functional for you and those you share it with.

Special Use Cases

What else might you use the room for? Your space should uniquely fit your needs. For example, If you or someone in your family is a musician, you may want a dedicated space to practice an instrument or store music. If a book club is your thing, seating that comes out or tucks away at a moment's notice will be useful. Think about your special-use cases and make note of these so we can employ them in our space-planning and furniture-selection sections.

> **Note about pianos:**
>
> Many clients tell me they want a piano but do not understand all the implications of including one in their design. As the daughter of a music teacher and pianist, I recognize how wonderful it is to have a piano in your home. Despite that, I only recommend getting a piano in two scenarios:
>
> - You or someone in the home actively plays the piano and enjoys it.
> - You have a specific space that lends itself to a piano, like a large area of the room that would not otherwise have furniture, or an alcove in the space that is the right size for the piano you want.

If you do have some who plays piano in your home, make this a priority in space planning, which we will tackle in the next chapter. Make it fabulous and useful. If you are just hoping that you'll have a piano player or if you simply have a romantic idea about having a piano in your home, I urge you to pass on it.

Placing a piano of any size in the room significantly impacts its layout, not only because of the space it inhabits but also because of the limitations in placement. A piano should not be placed too close to a window or heat source because it should be kept at an ideal humidity to maintain the instrument. The acoustics of the room must also be considered when placing a piano, which may require incorporating noise-reducing panels. It must be beautiful, of course, so you need to consider how the piano looks from different angles in the room and in which direction the bench and player should face.

You may think I am being over-the-top on these piano placement rules, but if you or someone in your home plays piano, these things matter. If they do not, don't waste the space and energy it takes to make a piano look good in your living room.

At this point you've stretched your brain to consider everything your space can be, how the space is and will be used, and what other needs you may have. This knowledge will be extremely useful as you put together an ideal layout in the next chapter.

Chapter 2 To-Do List

- Imagine all the possibilities
- Note future possible room changes
- Consider how you use the space
    - Who uses it
    - What time of day
    - Which activities
    - Storage needs
    - Problems to solve
    - Special-use needs

Chapter 3

Mapping Your Space

Now that you've thought about the ways you may use the space, it is time to put the pieces together. Creating a floor plan is an easy step to overlook, especially if you're already living in the space. But by creating a floor plan, you may discover something you had not considered before.

You do not need a degree in architecture to accurately measure and map your space. I'll give you a few guidelines, and it should not take much more than an hour to complete. You will need a tape measure that is long enough for your space, graph paper, and a pencil with a good eraser. Graph paper, image notations, and layout examples are included in the *Living Room Measuring and Layout Guide,* which you can download and print for free at LivingRoomLayout.com.

While I use space planning applications regularly in my business, I don't recommend you use them for the purpose of designing one room. Most of the planning applications require pricey subscriptions or come loaded with distracting artificial intelligence (AI) designers that don't provide reliable results. You will save time by sticking with the good old-fashioned hand-drawn method.

Measure and Draw Your Space

Do not worry if you find this to be initially confusing; it will make more sense as you do it. The purpose is to give you a bird's eye view of the space, not to have a perfect architectural drawing.

1. Start with your graph paper in landscape (width-wise) orientation. You will begin your drawing at the top left corner of the paper, leaving a square or two for space.

2. Measure the longest continuous wall in the space. Draw a line in pencil, using two graph paper squares per foot of space measured.

3. Determine if this scale will work for your room. If it is too long for the paper, adjust the line to reflect one square per foot. If the line is small on the page using this scale, increase it to reflect three or even four squares per foot.

4. Working clockwise, measure the total length of the next wall. If at this point you find your previous scale doesn't fit or is too small, you can erase your work and start over. Professional designers do it all the time!

5. Repeat step two for the next two walls. In most cases this will complete the measurement of the perimeter of the room. If your space is an unusual shape with

more walls, measure and draw those on the graph paper accordingly.

6. Return to the first wall you measured. Are there any windows, doors, or other fixed objects that should be noted? You will draw them on the floor plan using the following notations, also shown on the *Living Room Measuring and Layout Guide*, which you can download for free at LivingRoomLayout.com:

   a. Windows are drawn by making a thin rectangle where it is placed on the wall.
   b. Doors are drawn as one-quarter of a pie, using the right angle showing which direction the door opens.
   c. For an opening, simply erase that area of the wall.

   Start by measuring the distance from the corner of the wall to the left side of the fixed object. Even though you're using a scale, it is helpful to write this dimension next to the line. Measure the width of the door or window, and make the drawing that length. Finally, measure the distance from the right edge of the fixed object to the next corner (or fixed object if applicable).

7. Repeat step 6 until you have gone clockwise around the room.

8. Go back to the first wall and see if there is anything else to make note of on your plan. Anything that would impede furniture placement, such as radiators, vents, or built-in cabinetry, should be noted.

9. If you have furniture you'd like to use in the final design, note the dimensions below the drawing.
10. Make several copies of your drawing in order to try different layouts.

Determine Your Layout

To determine your ideal room layout, think about the focal point of the room, which you will build your seating around. If you have a fireplace, that is the focal point, whether you like it or not. Unless you plan to demolish it (which I rarely recommend), you'll need to work with it.

For most of us, the focal point is the TV, and it would be foolish to pretend otherwise. If the room is going to be used for TV viewing, build your seating around the TV.

Photography by Bartholomew Studio

> **Note about televisions and fireplaces:**
>
> If you have both a TV and fireplace, choosing a focal point can be a bit tricky. For almost two decades I've been trying to reconcile the fact that I want the fireplace, not the TV, to be the focal point. I have tried many different approaches, but I have learned that it's best to hang the TV over the fireplace. In some cases, I modify the facade or lower the mantel so the TV can be hung at the appropriate height. If this makes you cringe, I understand. It's not the only solution, but it's one I want you to strongly consider to make space planning easier. No need to worry about how it looks because you will make it beautiful—more on that in the next chapter.

In this chapter you will find a table listing furniture options with their customary dimensions and guidelines for furniture layout. The exact furniture you select will likely differ in size, but these dimensions will allow you to formulate a plan without being bogged down by specifics. With your focal point in mind, use the table and guidelines to come up with a few different primary seating options. These are the groupings of furniture that you think will be used the most. In most cases, the seating will include a sofa (or sofas) or a sectional, a center table (also known as a coffee table), and possibly some chairs. Do not include side tables or accent furniture at this point.

If this is the first time you've drawn a room to scale and placed furniture, you're probably feeling a little unsure of what to do and may even be frustrated, but don't worry. You can't screw this up (yet). Experiment, experiment, experiment! The only thing you need to do is play with it. It doesn't matter if you draw the sofa in the doorway—you're obviously not going to leave it there. The point is just to start arranging things.

Typical Furniture Dimensions

Piece of furniture	Common dimension (in inches)
Sofa	86 wide by 40 deep
Large sofa	92 wide by 40 deep
Loveseat	72 wide by 36 deep
Small L-shaped sectional	105 wide by 87 deep
Large L-shaped sectional	123 wide by 105 deep
U-shaped sectional	145 wide by 115 deep
Lounge chair	36 by 36
Chaise lounge	36 by 60

Soft Rules for Furniture Layout

Room Area	Dimensions for space
Conversation area	About 8 ft. wide
Space to walk through seating (i.e., distance between a sofa and chair)	Minimum 20 in. and ideally 24 in. or more
Distance from seating to coffee table	Minimum 12 in. to about 18 in.
Walkway	Minimum 28 in. and ideally 36 in. or more

As you move these items around in your space, gather information about the specific furniture you will be shopping for. For example, you may see that a narrower sofa would work better in your space, or you may determine that you have room for extra deep seating. Example layout suggestions are included in the free *Living Room Measuring and Layout Guide* at LivingRoomLayout.com.

> **Note about using your existing furniture:**
>
> If you like what you have, use it! It is important to confirm that it fits nicely in the space. If it does not fit, or if you don't like it, I urge you to open your mind to the idea of purchasing something new. This may be a hard pill to swallow, but furniture that is too big or too small for the space never looks right.
>
> Whenever I've tried to work with something that wasn't quite right, it has actually costs more in the long run. It wasn't worth spending more time and effort to find other things that worked with it, and in the end we often replaced the original piece.
>
> Even if you have a layout that works well with your existing furniture, it never hurts to put together a layout with different pieces. You may find that something clicks, and that may lead to a better result. Or it may give you more confidence in using the furniture you already have.
>
> For that reason it is worth confirming that you already have the best setup, even if you ultimately stick with the layout you are currently using.

Now that you have played around with the layout, narrow your layouts down to at least two, but no more than three plans. We will add to these plans to determine which is best and create the most special space for you.

> **Amy's Favorites**
>
> Obviously, not all layouts work in all spaces, but if you're stuck, try one of my favorites. There are few things more pleasing to the eye than a pair of sofas facing each other, in my opinion. If a pair of sofas is out of the question, I love a balanced sectional: either a U-shaped sectional with chaise lounges on either side or an L-shaped sectional offset by a pair of chairs.

Create a Nook

The key to creating a design that feels special is to create visually pleasing vignettes throughout the space. One way to do this is to add what I call a nook, which does not necessarily need to be a recessed area, though it can be. It is a spot in the room that adds beauty and often comfort.

Look at your top two to three floor plans and determine where you could put your nook.

If you have an alcove, that is an ideal spot. If not, consider corners or long stretches of walls to determine if there is an appropriate area for your nook. Adding beautiful storage pieces can be a good way to create this space.

Built-in Bookcases

Clients often want built-in bookcases, and designers love to integrate them. This special touch allows you to personalize a room and make it feel polished and comfortable. What I love most about built-ins is that I can tailor the storage to the client's needs.

We moved when our first child was five weeks old, and I spent countless hours breastfeeding on the couch in the unfinished family room while staring at a sad TV on an Ikea bookcase. This gave me plenty of time to envision what this room could look like. I decided that a built-in bookcase was just the way to create a moment on that wall, and it would also contain the mass chaos of baby toys floating around the room.

I got a quote from a cabinet company, and it really derailed my enthusiasm. While sticker shock would normally have slowed me down, I was spending most of my time in that one room and needed a change. It was all I could do not to cry as I looked around the unfinished space. I searched far and wide and got a referral for a guy who had just started a contracting business. He did not have the experience that most have, but I was willing to work with him to get the job done.

I scoured the internet and found pictures that showed exactly what I wanted. I knew the unit needed to go all the way to the ceiling, that it should have crown molding (wood trim at the ceiling) at the top and a false back in the middle section so the TV could sit slightly forward instead of directly against the wall. I wanted the lower cabinets to have as much interior space as possible without protruding too far into the room. I did not care what kind of wood they were made of because the whole thing would be painted. Plywood would be fine.

The day the contractor finished the cabinet was one of the greatest days I can remember. After he left and our baby was asleep, I ran downstairs like a kid who had just heard the ice cream truck. I picked up my daughter's bouncy chair and put it in one of the cabinets. On the next shelf, I arranged the books neatly in order of height. Below that, I placed a basket full of primary-colored toys. I closed the cabinet doors and a sense of peace and joy washed over me, as my living room once again felt like a place for adults.

When our daughter, and later our son, became toddlers, they knew where to put their toys. That is not to say they put them away, of course, but they knew there was a place just for their things, and that made everyone happy. Sure, my son would throw things in those cabinets like he was training to pitch for the Philadelphia Phillies, but it was plywood, so that did not matter. My kids also liked to get inside those cabinets from time to time, another benefit of making them as large as possible.

Looking back, the quality of that built-in cabinet is not what I would choose for the house I live in today, but it was absolutely right for that house and that moment in time. It emphasizes the point that only you can determine what makes the most sense for your needs.

Built-in cabinetry is a smart investment in most rooms. You may spend more on cabinetry than furniture, but it makes a beautiful statement and adds value to your home. The decision to add cabinetry often comes down to budget, so getting a quote is essential. Meet with a contractor, ideally one whose work you've seen, and follow the steps below to get the best result.

Exercise: Create a Plan for Built-in Carpentry

- Create a document that describes what you want and need out of built-in cabinetry.
- Add a photo of a built-in you like and note if you would change any aspects.
- Specify which details you expect, such as a door style, molding detail, or a specific finish. If you are unclear, it will slow down your quote. Make strong choices for the purpose of the estimate; you can always make changes before work begins.
- Print the document so the contractor can write on it and keep a copy.
- Determine the size you need with the contractor onsite. In order to make it feel generous, it should span from wall to wall or from corner to door opening. The unit should go from floor to ceiling, which makes it feel polished.
- Consider electrical needs. We will evaluate electrical needs more in an upcoming chapter, but let the contractor know that illumination and outlets may be required for this job.

- Ask by what date you can expect the estimate.
- Follow up with an email a day or two before you expect the estimate with the document attached. Contractors appreciate reminders.

I highly recommend getting three quotes for any project if for no other reason than to confirm the general cost.

If you feel comfortable with one of the contractors and you receive a timely professional estimate that is within your budget, book it!

If you get a bad feeling about a contractor, don't receive an estimate in a reasonable period of time, or get an unprofessional vibe, don't waste your time! Lose that number and call someone else.

> **Note about ready-made cabinetry:**
>
> You can get a built-in look by purchasing ready-made cabinetry. Most of the time, though, the juice is not worth the squeeze. Many companies sell units, sometimes modular so they can be pieced together, that can give you the look of built-ins. The problem with these units is that because they aren't customized to your room, the cabinets will not go to the ceiling (they wouldn't fit in the room in one piece if they did!), and will not cover the exact length you need. You can get close, though. Please consider all of the costs prior to ordering a ready-made unit, including shipping and assembly. If the cost is more than 50 percent of a custom unit, I recommend you save for the real thing.

Other Storage Ideas

You can create storage in other ways besides built-in cabinetry. Your room may benefit from the addition of a closet or a window seat with storage. Many rooms can have quirks—a strange closet here, an odd opening there. Often homes built in the '90s have room for TVs the size of a small car. I don't see that as a problem; I see it as an opportunity! You can create a really cool look with something simple, like an arch.

One client's home included a room with a built-in so deep it could fit a twin-sized bed. As I was taking my first stab at the floor plan, I thought about finding some antique doors to create a deep closet for blankets and games. I searched everywhere but could not find doors that were the right size. I moved on to high-quality new doors with a carved detail. My client liked the idea, but even though the budget was generous, the doors were expensive and required us to sacrifice in other areas.

One day my client sent me a picture, and I knew it was the way to go. It was simple: an opening to a closet-sized area with an arch. On the back wall was a piece of art, illuminated by a picture frame light, hanging over a beautiful dresser. It was just a regular piece of furniture, but the architecture made it appear to be a high-end custom piece.

We had the contractor come out and build the arch and install the light. It cost a fraction of what the doors would have cost and became a feature of the home.

If a built-in isn't right for you, but you would like to incorporate some storage furniture, consider what else works in your space and note it on your layout page.

Add Accent Furniture

Once you have placed your primary seating and storage, create a few placeholders for accent furniture. Accent pieces can include end tables, accent chairs, storage pieces, a console table, or floor lamps. A few squares and circles will do the trick, and the sizes are approximate for now. General guidelines for accent furniture and their typical dimensions are as follows:

Accent Furniture Typical Dimensions

Piece of furniture	Common dimension (in inches)
Square side table	Between 18 and 24
Round side table	Between 12 and 20
Floor lamp	20-inch circle or two 12" circles to denote an arched lamp
Console table	Between 36 and 72 wide and between 12 and 18 deep
Accent chairs	Between 18 and 36 square

With some solid layouts in mind, we are *almost* ready to start selecting furniture! Before we do that, though, we need to address something very important: lighting. Most people who don't work with a designer, and even some who do, fail to properly consider the light in their space, but you are going to use lighting to make your space look fantastic.

Chapter 3 To-Do List

- Map the layout of the space.
- Determine primary seating needs.
- Try multiple layouts using common furniture sizes.
- Select your favorite two or three primary seating concepts.
- Add a nook to each layout.
- If custom cabinetry is right for your room, get quotes.
- Create placeholders for accent furniture on each layout.

Chapter 4

Lighting and Electrical Plan

P eople often ask me to give them a good paint color. It is the request I loathe most in design because, depending on the lighting, paint looks different in every room. Once we get your lighting right, the wall color becomes almost irrelevant.

You may think you don't need to change your lighting or that you don't have the budget to hire an electrician. Many clients are reluctant on this topic, but having a lighting and electrical plan in place will not only help you create a professional-looking space, it may also save money in the end.

Lighting must be considered before you move on in your planning. In the event that you need to add or remove wiring for lighting, it will need to be done before you do anything to the walls.

Lighting Plan

Designing a lighting scheme may seem technical and complicated, but the truth is that you already have a lighting design, you just may not have thought about it. Consider all the electrical options in your room and how to tweak your design to make your finished space look polished.

To start, copy the outline of your floor plan onto another sheet of graph paper. You may be able to outline it if your paper is thin enough, or just sketch it lightly. It does not need to be as precise as the floor plan we used for the layout.

Use a pencil to plot any existing overhead lighting. Use the following instructions for each notation. Images are also included in the *Living Room Measuring and Layout Guide,* which you can download and print for free at LivingRoomLayout.com.)

- For a recessed light, draw a small circle with a cross through it.
- For an overhead light fixture (including chandeliers, flush mount, and semiflush mount lights), draw a large circle with a cross through it.
- For a fan, draw a large circle using a dotted line. Inside the circle, draw three rectangles to represent fan blades.
- Look at each wall and note other electrical items where they roughly appear in the room.
- If you have outlets in the floor, make a note of them on the floor plan.

- If you plan to eliminate anything currently in place, draw an *x* through it for now. You may use that wire for something else, so don't erase it yet.

Overhead Lighting

The goal is an evenly lit room with no shadows, and overhead recessed lighting (lights in the ceiling) works best to achieve it.

If you already have recessed lighting, turn it on and check for dark spots. If you find any, make a note on your plan and ask your electrician for help. If you have track or surface-mounted lights, replace them with recessed lights for the best effect.

If you don't have recessed lighting, install it. Recessed lighting is an element that will make all other aspects of your room look better, so it is well worth the expense. I'd rather you spend less on furniture to install recessed lighting, and that's a big statement from a designer! It will change the look of your room at night and can even make less expensive furniture look better. Also, installing recessed lighting isn't as invasive as it used to be.

On your electrical plan, plot where overhead lights will go. These lights look best in neat rows, four to six feet from the wall. In a room with a standard ceiling height, space the rows four to six feet apart. I recommend six to eight recessed fixtures in a typical living room.

If your ceiling is very high, you'll need to place the lights closer together. Consult your electrician for advice. For now, place the lights as described above and have your electrician adjust them.

Note about angled ceilings:

If you have angled ceilings, lucky you! That probably means you have high ceilings, too. High ceilings open up a world of possibilities for lights. For recessed lighting, your electrician can help you find the right lights to be placed on an angle.

High ceilings, angled or otherwise, also allow for eye-catching chandeliers. Most chandeliers utilize a standard canopy and chain system, which can be installed on an angle if need be. Stay away from light fixtures with straight downrods or large canopies. Make sure your light fixture will have a long enough chain for those tall ceilings of yours!

If you want to hang a chandelier from the center of the room where the angles meet, you'll need to modify the ceiling to create a flat space. This is not a complicated construction project, but it may require a carpenter. You can also consider adding multiple faux beams to get a distinguished-looking space and a flat surface for your light.

Amy's Favorites

I recommend a recessed light with a diameter of five or six inches. Smaller lights are available, but I don't recommend them unless necessary. The smaller lights create a more narrow beam angle which means more lights are required to illuminate dark spots. I typically use a baffle trim (which has a ribbed interior) for the trim style. I like it because it reduces glare, but a reflector or open style will get the job done too.

Decorative Lighting

Decorative lighting is a common feature in upscale designs, and it easily elevates a space. The styles include chandeliers, flush-mount or semiflush-mount lights, sconces, and picture frame lights. Once you have read through the options, add any type you would like to use without worrying about the exact fixture style or size yet.

Chandeliers are the most obvious type of fixture, but because they are primarily used in dining rooms, they are sometimes the least obvious choice for a living room. If your ceilings are more than nine feet tall, this type of fixture may work for you and bring your design to the next level. A hanging fixture, like a chandelier, can make a seating area feel intentional, especially if it is floating on a rug in the room. It should be placed directly over the coffee table in most cases. Think about your sightline before adding a chandelier; it should not block the TV, a window, or other room features.

> **Note about open floor plans and hanging fixtures:**
>
> Open floor plans often put a living area adjacent to the dining area, which can wreak havoc on your lighting plan. While I occasionally use two hanging fixtures in a row, I typically add a chandelier in the dining area and either a flush-mount or semiflush-mount fixture in the living area. Sometimes I eliminate the living area fixture completely and rely only on the recessed lights. Look at

> your room and determine what works best, prioritizing the dining fixture in the lighting plan.

Flush-mounted or semiflush-mounted lights are designed to either sit flush with the ceiling or close to the ceiling so they can be used in standard-height spaces, and they add interest in rooms without high ceilings. Like chandeliers, flush- or semiflush-mount fixtures usually work best centered over a seating area. If your room has a vestibule-type area or similar space, this is another nice place to use this type of fixture.

Sconces, which are lights that are mounted on the wall, can create a high-end designer moment in your room. Look at each wall and determine if there is a spot for a sconce or multiple sconces. Placing a pair of sconces above a fireplace is visually satisfying and useful. A single sconce, added to a nook of some kind, can add a great ambiance, especially when placed over a counter area or in a reading space.

Adding sconces on a long stretch of wall where you plan to put a piece of furniture or hang art makes the room feel well-designed. Blank walls look unintentional, but walls with lighting make a space feel elevated. I typically use a pair of sconces over a piece of furniture, but sometimes a single sconce or even a series of sconces fits the bill. If you have a built-in bookcase or are planning to add one, installing downlight sconces on the face of the piece adds a luxurious touch.

Picture frame lights are like sconces, but designed so the light points directly down to showcase a wall hanging. Adding a picture frame light or a series of lights over a gallery wall of photographs can really take a room to the next level. If you have a long stretch of wall that you'd like to use for this application, mark it on your electrical plan.

Placing a picture frame light over a single piece of art can also elevate your space. As you look around, determine if a large piece of art would fit on any of the walls. If so, add a picture frame light to your electrical plan.

Accent Lighting

Interior designers use lighting to add warmth and dimension to a design, and you can too. In addition to decorative lights, accent lighting will enhance your space. If any of these accent lighting ideas make sense for your design, mark it on the electrical plan.

Bookcase lighting. Illuminating a bookcase from within gives a room a luxurious feel. Whether you already have a bookcase in your space or are building a new piece, this design trick is worth incorporating. In recent years LED lighting has changed the game, and electricians are able to illuminate shelves in ways we have never seen before.

Illuminated architectural molding can create a glamorous look by lighting the woodwork. If you like the look of it, use inspiration photos to determine how you'd like it to look and make sure the electrician can deliver that concept.

Pin lights is a catchall term for lights that are typically installed in a ceiling to direct light onto a specific feature, adding a sophisticated element to your space. Pin lights usually highlight a piece of art, but I have seen them successfully installed to highlight molding, fireplace facades, or other architectural features.

Now that you have considered the key accent lighting options, note if any of them appeal to you and are worth incorporating into your plan. You can always eliminate them after you get the quote from the electrician!

Ceiling Fans

Do you *really* want a ceiling fan? Yes, they're essential for some people, especially in warmer climates, but I have never seen one that looks as good as a chandelier. If you primarily use air conditioning to cool your living room, consider ditching the fan. If you must have one, draw it on your floor plan, likely in the center of the space, and read on.

Fans present a challenge because they are not inherently beautiful and can interfere with the other light in the room. Work with your electrician to prevent the downcast of light from being too close to the blades (sometimes known as the strobing effect).

I recommend selecting a ceiling fan without an overhead light unless recessed lighting is out of the question.

Switches

Light switches might seem like a small detail, but it's important to consider in advance. Your electrician will ask about placement and function of the light switches, and these are not decisions to make on the fly.

Light switches generally come as either a one-way switch, also known as a single pole, or a three-way switch. A one-way switch is simple and turns a light on or off from one location. A three-way switch can turn a light on or off from two different locations. In my opinion, it should be called a two-way switch, but they did not consult me when naming it.

To determine which you need, consider where you will enter and exit the room most frequently. I always ask my clients which path they take when going to bed at night because that will tell us where there must be a switch. Note that spot on your electrical plan. If another location should have a switch as well, note it on the plan as a three-way switch..

If you already have switches in the desired locations, great! If you only have one and would prefer a three-way switch, get a quote from the electrician to add one.

Dimmers

I always recommend clients use dimmer switches. I have dimmer switches in every room of my house, including my closet and pantry. They are one of the greatest upgrades of all time: For less than ten dollars each, dimmer switches give you the ability to adjust the lights exactly to your desired level.

If you're interested in adding some luxury to your switches, I recommend Lutron dimmer switches. These switches allow you to set the lights at a certain level and then press the middle button to return to that level anytime you please.

When you turn off a Lutron switch, the light doesn't just go off, it gently fades out. I cannot explain the joy this gives me. !

As of this writing, I have mixed, and mostly bad, opinions of smart dimmer switches. I am especially skeptical of products sold on Amazon that look good but are *much* less expensive than the well-known brands. I have tried a few of these smart dimmer switches, but they have not performed very well. It seems like a small investment, but by the time you pay the electrician to install and perhaps uninstall the switches, it really adds up. Even trusted Lutron's smart system has bugs that are still being worked out. The technology just hasn't quite caught up, in my opinion. I hope to update this book soon with a recommendation for a reliable smart switch.

Lightbulbs

I recently read in the trade publication *Business of Home* that some designers are stockpiling incandescent light bulbs, whose production was banned in 2023. I understand why some designers are reluctant to make the switch to LED bulbs because the technology is still evolving. However, LED bulbs are better than incandescent bulbs in many ways, not the least of which is that they do not need to be replaced as frequently as traditional bulbs. Use these tips for selecting LED bulbs:

- Choose bulbs that have a color temperature of around 3,000 K to get warm light like an incandescent bulb. (This number will be listed on the box. The color temperature of light bulbs is based on a measurement called a kelvin, K.)

- Choose bulbs that are dimmable and that have the warm dim feature. This feature makes the light become warmer (more orange) as it dims, just like the light of incandescent bulbs do, rather than just cutting the amount of light in the room.
- Pay careful attention to the wattage or lumens suggested on your fixtures. Using the wrong wattage or lumen was less consequential with traditional bulbs, but LEDs flicker when the wrong wattage is used.

To complete your lighting design, I suggest the following common bulbs:

The Standard E26 base light bulb is used in most lamps and comes in a variety of shapes and finishes. The *E* stands for Edison screw and refers to the specific base type, and the number refers to the diameter of the base in millimeters. I recommend stocking up on classic white frosted bulbs for most applications.

The E12 base light bulb is smaller than the E26 bulb, considered candelabra size, and what you'll need for most chandeliers and sconces. If your bulbs are exposed, like on most chandeliers, opt for clear. If your bulbs are covered, perhaps with shades, use a frosted bulb to prevent shadow from coming through the interior of the shades.

Some light fixtures require unique bulbs, so when purchasing your lights, take a look at the description to see what kind of bulb is needed.

Many different shapes of bulbs are available, and an unusual shape can make a beautiful statement on certain fixtures. You may choose to use small round bulbs on certain sconces or tall skinny bulbs in a chandelier. Sometimes I will order an oversized bulb to give a flush mount light a really unique look. Take it case by case, and if you aren't sure, stick with the classics.

> **Amy's Favorites**
>
> If you aren't sure what type of lighting you want, the following formula always works!
>
> 1. Install recessed lighting that flushes the entire room with light.
> 2. Add a pair of sconces or a picture frame light somewhere in the space, possibly in the nook.
> 3. Put everything on a dimmer.

Other Electrical Elements

While we are at it, let's consider other electrical elements that will increase your room's function, such as media and electrical outlets.

Media

Most people have a TV in their family room or living room, but if you don't have or want a TV, feel free to skip this section.

You've likely already identified where you'll place your TV in the floor plan, so you must make sure you have the right electrical outlet to get it there. A polished living room usually has a wall-mounted TV. The outlet should be placed roughly 50 inches from the ground so the TV covers it. A quad outlet (four receptacles) or a duplex (two receptacles) with an integrated USB port will provide access to any systems you may add.

Most new installations use Wi-Fi-enabled systems (Apple TV, Roku, Amazon Fire TV Stick) to hook up the TV, but I still ask the electrician to run an ethernet cable for a direct hookup if possible. No one wants to wait for buffering. If you have cable, be sure to have the wire placed near the electrical outlet..

> **Note about putting televisions on furniture:**
>
> Occasionally clients want to avoid hanging their TVs, but this is one area I do not compromise on. You have already spent too much time planning a beautiful room to ruin it with an ugly TV on a stand! In the past, mounting a TV was complicated and expensive, but today it is something that can be easily achieved with a twenty-dollar mount and a YouTube video. If you aren't up to hanging it yourself, you will find many handymen who will do it for a reasonable price.

Television size

Some people roll their eyes when I say this, but bigger truly is better in this instance. The TV size should be proportional to the space, of course, but I recommend the biggest TV that fits comfortably in that space. A quick calculation of the available space as outlined in this table will guide you.

Recommended TV Size Based on Available Space	
Space with strict size limits, e.g., over a fireplace (all measurements in inches)	On an open wall (all measurements in inches)
Measure available width and deduct 8. Pick a TV size that best fits in the remaining space. For example: If your available space measures 72 total width, subtract 8 and find a TV that measures 64 wide or less. TVs are measured diagonally, so a 65 TV is actually about 57 wide.	Determine the distance between your viewing location and where the TV will be placed and divide that number in half. For example, if the distance between your sofa and your TV wall measures 120, then look for a TV with a diagonal width of 60. Use this formula as a guide, not a rule. You may find one size up or down is a better fit for your needs.

Television selection

I recommend the same TV in every room I design: The Frame TV by Samsung. The Frame looks like a piece of art when it is not being used but functions as a regular TV when on. It sits very close—less than one inch—from the wall. I always add an actual frame to The Frame TV for extra polish. While many clients have been skeptical of The Frame's ability to provide a great picture and viewing experience, none have ever been disappointed.

The challenge with The Frame TV is that because it is so thin, its "brain" lives outside the unit and requires special electrical work, as well as a place to house it, so make sure the person installing The Frame understands what needs to be done.

I have not yet found another TV that offers what The Frame offers, which is why I have mentioned it by name. I hope that other companies get on board with this concept soon. If you opt against The Frame, look for a TV that is inconspicuous: the thinner the better—less frame, more screen. You get the picture (pun intended).

Sound

I wish all TVs had excellent sound and did not require additional speakers! Some people think external speakers are essential to the viewing experience, and although I didn't want to include a section about external speakers (which can detract from design) in this book, I had a nightmare that after spending money to beautifully finish your room, someone would make an eleventh-hour demand that you place hideous speakers everywhere. For that reason, I decided to get ahead of it and add some advice so you can determine what type of sound system makes sense for your room while you are in the design process.

When working on a client's living room, I agreed to use the client's audiovisual (A/V) guy for simplicity. With so many details in this renovation, sound was low on my priority list, so I just asked him to "make the speakers as invisible as possible." He said, "I'll see what I can do." I envisioned speakers integrated into the ceiling with inconspicuous covers painted to match.

After the speakers were installed, the client asked me what I thought of them. I looked around and could not find a single one. He laughed as I looked around, and then he turned on the sound. There was true stereo-quality surround sound, but the speakers were, well, invisible. The A/V guy had found an incredible new system with speakers in the ceiling that were imperceptible. I was blown away!

The client was very happy, but he did tell me that their son's room was above the living room and that it was quite loud in there, so there was a drawback. At this time the technology is too new to recommend here, but it is very promising! Perhaps someday my dream of invisible speakers everywhere will come true.

To determine what kind of sound you want in your space, answer the following questions:

- What would you like for your sound system? Is the sound coming through the TV adequate? If so, there is no need to complicate things. If not, is surround sound important to you? Do you need a subwoofer for the bass?

- How much are you willing to invest in sound? If sound is a priority, call a local A/V store and get a quote for an integrated sound system. Integrated speakers (i.e., in the ceiling) are always the most aesthetically pleasing. If you'd like to save some money here, consider stand-alone options like Sonos speakers. Asking your electrician to install outlets high in your room so you can plug them in there may be the most cost-effective option.

- Will your sound be hooked up to a larger system? While hiring a consultant from an A/V store may be your best option for complex systems, there are options that you can bring in yourself.

Once you have determined which audio and visual choices are best for you, note these on your electrical plan.

> **Note about sound bars:**
>
> Sound bars are speakers designed to project excellent quality sound into a room without the necessary work required to install surround sound. Sound bars typically sit beneath a TV, and while they're better than many of the alternatives, they still aren't very attractive. A sound bar underneath a mounted TV can appear to be a TV on a stand. How sad!
>
> If you opt for a sound bar, place it far enough away from the TV so it does not look like one unit. Sound bars can also be mounted to the wall beneath the TV, again far enough away to make the distinction between the two units.

Outlets

With lighting and media decisions in place, you need to make sure electrical hookups exist in all the necessary places. While new homes and renovated rooms follow code for electrical outlets, that is no guarantee your room has an outlet where you want one. If your home is older, you may not have any outlets on some walls. Create an inventory of what you need and their ideal placement by answering the following questions and then noting your desired outlets on your floor plan:

- Where will you plug in lamps, chargers, and any other devices you would like easy access to?
- Do you have any special needs that require outlets?
- Would you like to have floor lamps or lamps on side tables placed in the middle of a room? If so, consider installing a floor outlet.

How do you feel after reading the first four chapters, mapping your space and creating an electrical plan? I find that every job, whether a simple room lift or a huge renovation, has a down point. It is the point where the initial excitement has diminished and you cannot see much progress. That down point frequently happens here because we have only worked on the technical aspects of your design so far. If you are feeling that way, I assure you it is about to get better! It's time to create a visual of what all of those technical things are going to look like together.

Chapter 4 To-Do List

- Sketch out the perimeter of your room to create your electrical plan.
- Assess your current lighting and determine which additions you will make.
- Hire an electrician.
    - Explain your goals for the space
    - Flush the room with light
    - Necessary outlets and/or Ethernet cables if applicable
    - Feature lighting if applicable
- Purchase materials
    - Television
    - Smart TV system or cable box if applicable
    - Sound equipment if applicable

Decorative light fixtures will be selected in a future chapter

Chapter 5

Creating Your Mood Board

People always tell me that they know what they like, but they don't know how to put it together. I understand this common frustration. Bringing ideas together can seem overwhelming, but a mood board, which is a compilation of images that represent your design, will allow you to sort through the things you love and pull the ideas together in a beautiful way.

Photography by Bartholomew Studio

Finding Inspiration

This is an exciting time to be a designer, with so many great ways to share ideas. When I'm working on a project and inspiration strikes, I immediately go online and look at images of what other people have done. The sea of inspiration helps me decide how to best execute my own idea.

While some great applications allow you to compile your ideas digitally, I find it works best to use good old-fashioned paper and scissors. To create a mood board for your room, you will first browse images, either digital or physical (e.g., online images, magazine or catalog pictures), to figure out what appeals most to you. Once the ideas are narrowed down, you will print them (or cut them out) in the variety of sizes listed in the next section. After you group images together, you will attach them to a piece of foam core board in order to get a good look at your overall design.

Keep in mind that you're not trying to find images to replicate but rather images to help you discover what you like most. As you sift through the different categories of ideas, follow these two rules:

- You must love it.
- It must honor your home.

By honoring your home, I mean you should select items that are in harmony with the overall style of your home. For example, most of my clients live in traditional homes but want to add a modern look to their space. If a client is drawn to an ultramodern chrome light fixture, I would recommend a similar style, but in brass. The metal will feel more cohesive with the home, but the modern style will still appeal to the client. You can have your cake and eat it too.

All these images are your inspiration images, and you will print them in a variety of sizes to arrange on your mood board.

Choose a Focal Point for Your Space

It's time to ask yourself a very important question: What makes your heart go pitter-patter? Every room needs a *star*, the item to which everything else in the room metaphorically bows. Sometimes the star is a special light fixture, unusual wallpaper, beautiful millwork, or a bold piece of furniture. Other things in the room can shine too—just not as brightly as the star.

As you look through your inspiration images, notice what your eye is drawn to in each room. Do you love rooms with large modern light fixtures, or does a cozy wall with wood trim appeal more to you? Is a vibrant wallpaper your favorite thing to look at or would you prefer to add a splash of color or a pattern on pillows? Look for trends in your taste—one of these ideas just might be your *star*.

Choose three images that represent a possible star in your room. Print each one on a standard-size piece of printer paper.

> **Note about choosing paint as you room's star:**
>
> While your paint color could be the star, I suggest choosing something else. I don't select the final paint colors until the end of the design process because the

possibilities are infinite. If there is a color you absolutely love, look for it in inspiring photos. You may fall in love with the idea of a purple couch or mustard yellow drapes! The color may end up on the walls, but start with it in something other than paint for your room's star.

Develop Other Categories

As you did with the star, look through your inspiration images and select at least three images in each of the following categories and sizes:

Category	Image print-out size (compared to piece of paper measuring 8.5" by 11")
Primary seating	½ page
Center table	½ page
Solid fabric or wallpaper	¼ page
Large-scale pattern *Fabric or wallpaper, for example, a large floral or geometric print.*	½ page
Small-scale pattern *Fabric or wallpaper, for example, a small check or stripe.*	¼ page
Window treatment	½ page
Accessories (choose 6 –12)	¼ page

Group Your Images

With the images in front of you, start by separating the three star images. Next, place one of your primary seating images next to each star. At least one combination will probably feel like it belongs together. If you don't see a perfect match, that's okay. Put them together as best you can and move on to the next step.

With these three piles in front of you, add a center table to each combination. If you see that one table is more fitting with one primary seating image, put them together. Do your best to pair all three combinations. Set aside these three piles.

The next step is to create three new piles, where you mix and match some pattern combinations. Some people want to know where the pattern will go in the room, but try not to focus on that. At this stage, you are just trying to get a vibe. Group one of your solid fabric or wallpaper images with one large-scale and one small-scale pattern. Do they look good together? If not, mix your options until they feel good enough. Some people find this part difficult, so if you struggle, don't worry. Simply pick your three favorite patterns and set the rest aside. If you want to add complementary fabrics as you go through these steps, feel free, but it is not necessary.

Next, merge your piles into three overall groups, each with a star, furniture, and a combination of patterns.

When I put together a mood board for a client, it does not always come together easily—or stay the same over time. I often rotate my selections and bring in substitutions. As long as you're working with images that excite you, the desired result will come.

Make It Official

Do you have a favorite combo out of the three sets? I bet you do. If you're not sure, remove one of the combos you put together and see how it makes you feel. I find that I can usually eliminate one or two groups at this point. Eliminate the group you are least excited about.

If you feel strongly about one, run in that direction! If not, make two mood boards instead of just one. I have done this both ways, and both can produce excellent results. Start by attaching the star in the center of the board. I use a hot glue gun, but tape works too. From there, place the primary seating to the left, grouping the coffee table with the sofa. On the right side of the star, place your pattern images with a slight overlap.

> **Note about using your star:**
>
> The star may appear in any element of your design, so once you have your star, allow it to supersede other choices in that category. Trust your decision, and do not worry because we will refer back to the mood board every step of the way, and all future decisions will be cohesive with it.

Add Interest and Texture

Your board will still have a fair amount of white space, so use your other images to fill in the concept. Hold each window treatment and accessory up to your board(s), and if one feels right, stick it on! You may not end up using these exact selections, but the exercise will guide you when it comes time to shop. Remember, these decisions aren't permanent, so give yourself permission to play.

> **Amy's Favorites**
>
> When I am having trouble figuring out what excites a client, I find that light fixtures can spark interest. Shades of Light is one of my favorite lighting retailers because it carries a wide range of fixture styles and price points. Go to the Shades of Light website and pick out a few light fixtures that you like—whether you think they are right for your space or not—and use them in a google image search. This will generate photos that include similar fixtures. These images will lead you to more images with similar design styles, and from there, you will have oodles of photos to add to your mood board.

Finishing your mood board is a huge step in this process. You have done all the things that lead to a fantastic result and make furniture selection will be a breeze.

Chapter 5 To-Do List

- Gather materials for your mood board.
- Browse images, choose three possible stars for your room, and cut or print them.
- Browse and select images in the other categories and cut or print them.
- Group your primary seating images together.
- Match each group with a star image.
- Group your pattern images together.
- Add each group of patterns to the previous group of images.
- Attach pictures to the board.

Chapter 6

Primary Seating

It is time to navigate the ever-changing world of home furnishings, and we'll start with primary seating selections. Don't worry—you've already done the homework, and I'll give you the tools to make sure it goes smoothly.

Using the photos on your mood board, look at the seating and figure out what you like best about the images you chose. Note the following seating characteristics:

- Number of seat cushions
- Style of cushions
- Style of back cushions (or lack thereof)
- Style of arm
- Height of arm
- Legs or skirt
- Height of back
- Detail (studs, contrast piping)

Write down the features that appeal to you. Knowing some design industry-specific lingo will help you know what you want. I've compiled the terminology of some common seating features below. Searching the internet for a similar sofa and reading a description will also help you determine the names of features to shop for.

Term	Feature or Style	Term	Feature or Style
Welt, also known as piping	Fabric or other material detail added at seams	Knife-edge cushion	Back cushion that tucks in the corners and attaches to a single welt
Tight-back sofa	Sofa with no back cushions	English arm	Arm that is low, rounded, and tucks on the side
Tufting	A stitching method that creates dimples (often covered by buttons) in upholstery	Track arm	Sofa arm that is straight
Bench cushion	Single cushion on sofa that goes across multiple seats	Nailheads	Metal studs added as a decorative detail, usually where welt would be

> **Note about back cushions:**
>
> Back cushions have a big impact on how your primary seating looks and a bigger impact on how it feels and wears. The cushions of lower-quality sofas (and believe me, I've owned a few) will lose shape over time and start to look sloppy. Even high-quality sofas require regular cushion rotation to keep them looking fresh.
>
> One solution I frequently use is to choose a sofa with a tight back—a sofa with no back cushion. I like tight-back sofas because there are no back cushions that need to be fluffed or rotated and it always looks tailored. Some people prefer a super cushy sofa, which a tight-back sofa lacks. My family likes it, though, because we have lots of throw pillows to sink into.

Budget

You may wonder how you can start selecting furniture without a budget in mind. My experience is that no one (myself included) actually knows how to budget for an entire room. I was trained to ask the budget question when first meeting a client, but in practice I find this sometimes limits the project because the client does not yet know what suits their needs. For this reason I suggest developing a budget as you go through the furniture selection process.

Budgets can vary a lot depending on how you plan to use your space. A few years ago a client asked me to design his formal living room. He wanted the room to look great because it was next to the front door, but he confessed that the family would rarely use it.

At the time, curved sofas were becoming popular. I had seen some at High Point Market (a large furniture trade show) and thought they were cool. As of this writing, they still are considered in vogue, but at some point in the future, I know its likely that someone will read this and laugh. Trust me, at the time they were in style!

I liked the idea of using something unique in this client's space, but it didn't think it made sense to spend big money on a custom upholstered piece. I went to my lower-cost sources and found an affordable brand that made a curved sofa. It may have been put together with cardboard and bubblegum, but we didn't care. It looked great and did the trick.

Choosing an affordable sofa gave me room in the budget to invest in fabulous art. We picked a piece that not only made the room look like a million bucks but will also appreciate in value. The client loves the way his funky living room looks, and he tells his friends that he actually made money by hiring an interior designer.

In general, plan to sped the most money on sofas and other upholstered primary seating, unless it wil not get frequent use. One way to look at the cost of seating is in terms of the number of seats. A standard sofa is really three chairs. A small sectional has five seats. When comparing pricing, I consider an L-shaped sectional as two sofas and a U-shaped sectional as three. This method can be useful when it comes to shopping because it wards off sticker shock for bigger pieces.

Browse for Your Primary Seating

Shopping in person is essential for selecting your furniture, even if you ultimately order it online. With your floor plan and notes in hand, you can use the salesperson as your assistant. They have a wealth of information and can easily locate the best pieces for you.

Browse in Tiers

In my mind, the furniture world can be divided into three tiers, with some overlap. The top tier is furniture from design showrooms, and while many of these brands are now available to consumers online, the ordering process usually isn't very user-friendly. These brands are set up as wholesalers, so you'll need to go to a high-end furniture store to shop these brands in person. Not all of us have the budget to order top-tier furniture, but all of us can browse there to see what we like.

Find a store that carries top-tier brands to see what appeals most to you. If you aren't sure where to go (they are not all created equal), search for nearby stores that carry luxury brands. A few of my favorites are Bernhardt, Wesley Hall, and Lexington. Perigold is an online store that carries many top-tier brands. Search Perigold's website to get a feel for what you like and learn which brands carry frames (the furniture shape) that appeal to you. Cross reference these brands with stores in your area to determine the best place for you to shop.

Going to one of these stores in person allows you to see and feel large fabric samples and drape them on the furniture to get a feel for how they look. Sit on many different pieces and determine what is most comfortable for you. Note the following details:

- Seat height
- Seat depth
- Back height
- Cushion fill and thickness

When you know which furniture you like at a top-tier store, note their prices, then use that information to continue your search at other price points. You may be surprised to find that in combination with other sales and promotions, some top-tier furniture is priced the same or is occasionally more affordable than lower tiers. Compare price and quality as you check lower tiers.

Second-tier furniture is found in what some people may call big-box stores, such as Ballard Designs, Pottery Barn, and Crate & Barrel. These stores provide custom upholstery but usually in a smaller selection of fabrics. Furniture from these stores is typically priced at a slightly lower price point than top-tier furniture. In general, the build of these pieces is good and dependable enough for high-traffic residential use.

Third-tier furniture is mass-manufactured, like the pieces you can order online or purchase at Target or Raymour & Flanigan. Typically these brands offer the fewest fabric options, the lowest price point, and also the lowest quality. Some second-tier brands like Pottery Barn or Crate & Barrel also carry a lower price line that is more like third-tier quality and pricing.

There is nothing wrong with third-tier furniture, and it may be the best choice for your living room. If you plan to move in a few years or the room will not get heavy use, third-tier furniture may be right for you. Use the information you gathered when shopping the top-tier brands to find the furniture that best meets your needs.

In design school we learned that high-quality upholstered furniture is made with a kiln-dried hardwood frame and with eight-way hand-tied springs. In practice, though, I find that the quality of the build is more dependent on other factors. Furniture made in the United States or Europe does make a difference in quality. Full disclosure: Most brands—even top-tier brands—assemble their furniture in the United States or Europe, but the frames are made in Asia. Even so, my personal experience is that those products are generally better quality than those that are made entirely in other parts of the world.

Fabric Selection

Primary seating is usually your workhorse and needs a true performance fabric. Look for fabrics with high *double rub* counts, which measure how long the fabric takes to wear.

Performance fabric should have a count of 50,000 or more. Textured fabrics are more forgiving over time, so search for options with subtle detail.

The look of the fabric matters a lot, of course, because this piece will take up a large portion of the space. A solid fabric in a color with neutral undertones works well for primary seating because it allows us to bring in a variety of accent colors elsewhere. I find browns, blues, and greys to be most useful, although a deep green or blush pink can read as a neutral as well. Use your mood board to determine what you like and also to gauge what works in the space.

Printed versus woven fabrics

For primary seating, we almost always want a woven fabric. In a woven fabric, the fibers go all the way through and when you turn it over you'll be able to see the color of the thread.

A printed fabric has ink or dye pressed into it to create a pattern. These types of fabrics are less resilient, though, because the dye is more likely to rub off over time. I do not recommend printed fabric for your primary seating. If you find a fabric you love that is printed, save it for pillows, accent seating, or ottomans.

> **Note about fabrics and artificial intelligence:**
>
> I am an early adopter and love all of the wonderful things that AI can do for us! Despite my enthusiasm, the technology around viewing fabrics is still in its infancy. A website may show you an image of what your fabric will look like on a piece of furniture, but that is sometimes counter-productive. Most of these programs do not

> understand pattern repeats or seaming, or how to correct for shadows. Most generated images are not good representations of what the finished product will look like. The good news is that they typically look worse than the actual item does, so you have nowhere to go but up! Trust your instinct over AI, at least when it comes to fabric selection.

Leather

I have a confession to make: I have never ordered a leather sofa for a living room. I just don't like leather sofas! I don't know where this leather aversion came from exactly, but I think it had something to do with the furniture I grew up with. That's for me and my therapist to sort out, but I felt obligated to let you know.

Clients sometimes request leather for durability, but it is not always as durable as it seems. Many different grades of leather exist, and the lower grades (which are not always at a lower price point) tend to degrade over time. I'm sure you've seen a cracked and flaky leather piece in a fraternity house or doctor's office waiting room at some point in your life. This flaw has more to do with the way the leather was treated than the actual material, but it's something to be aware of. If you're choosing leather for its durability, select a high grade with an antiqued finish.

For the most part, choosing leather means you're committing to brown or tan as a major element of your design. Brown shades are rising in popularity at the time of this writing, but they may not be the desired lead color in your design. While lots of other colors of leather exist, I generally reserve these colors for smaller applications like an ottoman or accent chair. The colors don't wear as well and look out of place on larger leather furniture.

> **Amy's Favorites**
>
> If you're feeling stuck when it comes to which furniture style is best for you, use these tips below, as they work in nearly all styles of homes and are available from most major brands.
>
> Choose a sofa or sectional with bench seating, a wide track arm, and no skirt. I love skirts on furniture but rarely order them on primary seating because they're a bit trendy and can be problematic with kids and pets. If you can get this style with a fixed base (meaning there is a piece of wood or metal that the legs are attached to that goes all the way across the base of the sofa), that's even better.
>
> For fabric, choose a performance velvet that has some texture. While I wish all sofas could be white, I've accepted the fact that almost none of them can be. It is just too impractical for most homes. For that reason choose a rich color like a taupe, chocolate brown, or navy.

Pillow Selection

Most primary seating will come with pillows, but they won't always be the best choice for the room. Pillows are a low-risk way to integrate color and pattern in the design, so use them as an opportunity to infuse something you love.

Some furniture brands allow you to select pillow fabrics, while others automatically include pillows in the same fabric as the sofa. The pillows that come with the sofa can be useful in tandem with patterned pillows, but sometimes they detract more from the sofa than enhance it.

A standard sofa looks best with four pillows in two different fabrics. One pair of these should be a somewhat bold or colorful pattern, and the other, a smaller pattern, either a texture or solid. Large square pillows look best, so if you have control over the pillow size, opt for those that measure 22 or 24 inches.

Look at your mood board patterns to determine if one of those should show up on a pillow. If so, use it as one of your choices and choose another pattern to coordinate with it. If the fabric is a pattern, consider adding a solid pillow in one of the colors from the fabric.

You aren't limited to what you put on the mood board, of course, but use it as your guide for choosing fabrics or pillows. If you're at a store and see a patterned pillow that appeals to you, first confirm it is cohesive with the mood board, and then if so, buy a pair! Use that pattern to locate the two additional solid or textured pillows for your sofa.

Pillows on a sectional can be arranged in a variety of ways. Start with six pillows and see how it feels. I generally start with the standard sofa layout and add complementary pillows at the corner. In addition to the four square pillows, I typically add a smaller rectangular pillow (usually 14 inches by 24 inches) and a larger solid or textured square.

Many online brands offer great-looking pillows, and I have been pleased with some selections at stores like Target and HomeGoods as well. If you want something more customized, Etsy has many sellers that offer pillows in designer fabrics or will make pillows to your specifications. This is also a great source to order solid or textured pillows in a generous size.

Pillow inserts feel best when they're made of down and feathers, and a trick is to order an insert that is a few inches larger than the pillow cover itself. This will give you a luxurious feel.

Confirm Measurements and Order

You have a floor plan, so you already know what size seating works in your space, but as the saying goes, *measure twice and cut once*. Before you finalize the order, bring home the measurements of the furniture you like and look at them in the space to confirm they will fit. I use blue tape on the floor to see where furniture will sit before placing an order.

Don't forget to also look at all the doors, hallways, or corners your furniture will need to travel through before it reaches its final destination. Look at the width of the largest piece and make sure it can clear all those spots. It is rare that a first-floor piece doesn't fit in a home, but if that is the case you'd rather discover it now than on delivery day!

You have jumped through a lot of hoops to get to this point, so you can place this order with confidence! You may not *feel* totally confident about it, but you have a floor plan that shows it fits and a mood board to show that it is cohesive.

Sometimes clients have trouble deciding between two somewhat similar pieces. This may sound silly, but if you're debating between two pieces that both fit and are cohesive in your design, flip a coin. How does the coin flip result make you feel? *You already know which one you want.* It is normal to second-guess your choice, but don't give yourself a migraine over the decision. Close your eyes, take a deep breath, and think about the furniture in your room. Then take a few minutes to make sure everything on the order is correct, place the order, and keep moving!

Now is a good time to check your party date. Make sure your furniture will arrive at least a week or two before your big day. You want to account for any delays and leave time for accessorizing.

Chapter 6 To-Do List

- Use your mood board to determine which features of primary seating you like best.
- Bring your floor plan and inspiration images to a furniture store to shop.
- Choose a fabric that is durable and cohesive with your plan.
- Confirm the measurements in your space.
- Confirm your furniture will be able to pass through the doors, hallways, and corners to get to your room.
- Review the order details.
- Place the order with confidence.

Chapter 7

Center Table Selection

Sometimes called a cocktail table (just to sound more chic, I suppose) or the more classic coffee table, the center table is a workhorse in any room, so you want something that will hold up. Plan to invest in it, though not to the extent of your primary seating.

A commanding center table sets the tone for a room. If you want to save money in this category, you may find success purchasing two identical coffee tables to cover the space you want rather than investing in a more expensive, larger table. Choose tables with square sides so they look like one unit.

Size

Size is the biggest factor here. Unfortunately, commercially made tables err on the side of being too small—even in smaller rooms. I rarely select a table that is less than 36 inches in either direction and even then, it can feel like a postage stamp. You already have an idea of what size works well in your room based on the floor plan, so use that dimension to find something that fills the space.

The height of the table is important too. The table's height ca change the feeling of your room, and getting it wrong will leave you on the phone with customer service begging for a return. The height of a standard coffee table is about 18 inches. In general, a slightly higher table will work and provide a more formal look. There is a limit to how tall it should be, though, and while sofas that sit higher can accommodate coffee tables as tall as 22 inches, when you exceed that height, it sometimes gets *weird*. I really wish I could explain this better, but both my degree in journalism and nearly two decades in design leave me at a loss for words. Tall coffee tables are just strange. I don't know how they get manufactured, but they do. Beware.

Stick to something no taller than 22 inches, and make sure it's at least 15 inches tall. You will find plenty of tables on the shorter side, especially with the recent explosion of the bohemian look in home design. There are tables that are only 12 inches tall, and at that height, you might as well put your drink directly on the floor. It's odd that they make them that short. My theory is that some manufacturers really latched on to this trend in order to save money on materials, but that is a discussion for another day. The proportions look perfectly normal online, but when the table arrives, you'll end up double-checking to see if you accidentally ordered the child-sized version.

A designer trick is to tuck ottomans in various places, and underneath the coffee table is a great place for this. You need at least 18 inches of clearance in order to nuzzle ottomans under a coffee table. While some tables with this type of clearance exist, a custom-built table ensures enough clearance without the coffee table being too tall for its own good. Etsy is a fantastic resource for custom-built tables because it gives you access to artisans who can build a table to your specifications.

Material

Your center table can add to or emphasize your design. For example, in a room full of upholstered furniture, a wood coffee table adds warmth. Use your material selection to fill out the look you want.

Wood is classic, and the market is flooded with both real wood and faux wood options. Either way, the material will wear with use, and the advantage of the real wood table is that you can always have it refinished. The disadvantage here is that refinishing your table may cost the same as a new table. Make your decision based on what appeals to you and how likely you are to want a new table in ten years.

Glass tables are great for a room where you want to keep things light. In a room with a bold pattern or heavy color, a glass table virtually disappears. Functionally, they are both excellent (think no water rings) and dangerous (think toddlers).

There are excellent tables made of alternative materials like metal or concrete. You must consider them on a case-by-case basis, of course, but if they work with your mood board, they could be an option with excellent longevity.

I am partial to a table wrapped in grass cloth, an option which has become more available recently. These tables provide a diverse color palette to choose from and add a natural texture to the room. Unfortunately, they're not very stain friendly. Sometimes they're coated in lacquer, which makes them better but not indestructible. For this reason, you may want to order a piece of glass to top it, which increases the durability and still gives us the look.

> **Amy's Favorites**
>
> I choose a table for its size and shape first, and after that, I usually look for something chunky. The heft gives the room a generous feeling. Tables made of wood or metal are best for durability. If you aren't sure, go with something that has visual weight to it. It does not actually need to be heavy, but it should look like it is.

As you narrow your selections, print or cut out your favorite images and hold them up to your mood board to see which complements the design best. That piece is the winner. Place the order and get ready for some fun: We choose lighting in the next chapter.

Chapter 7 To-Do List

- Use your floor plan to determine the best size table for your space.
- Consider what materials are most compatible with your design.
- Narrow down your selection to two or three tables that you like.
- Print photos and hold them up to your mood board.
- Order your table.

Chapter 8

Light Fixture Selection

You identified which type of fixtures you'd like in your room in chapter 4, and now you get to choose them! While going to a lighting store can give you some great information, the internet is going to be your best friend for this search. Viewing lights en masse can be overwhelming, and it is difficult to get a sense of what one single fixture might look like in your space. The internet has a much broader selection and conveniently allows you to narrow your search.

In the section below you will narrow your options by size first and then by style. For each category of light, choose two or three fixtures you like and print images of them to hold up to your mood board. Hold each image up to see what is most cohesive with the rest of the room and select one from there.

If you want to make room in your budget, lighting is an opportunity to do so. Don't get me wrong—high-end lighting is worth every penny and can really enhance a room—but given the choice between better quality seating and more elegant lighting, I'd choose seating every time. Luckily, you can find some beautiful fixtures and lamps that are affordable and get the job done.

Early in my career I was hired to redecorate a beach house. The house had seven bedrooms, and I wanted each one to have a unique personality. One of the rooms would be used by a little boy who was interested in sailing, so I let this guide my design. I don't like a room with an overbearing theme, but I love a hint of a theme. We decided that a nautical color palette and a few weathered buoys would do the trick.

The room needed a flush-mount light, and given that it was a kid's room and we had already used much of the budget, I went to Wayfair.com to see what I could come up with. I easily found a light; one that was modern with a sunburst detail that looked like a compass. I sent a picture to the client and we agreed it was perfect. Best of all, the price was incredible!

I ordered several more lights that day, along with some bedding and accent tables. This was one of many, many things that would be delivered to the house in time for my meeting with the electrician.

On the day of the installation I could hardly wait to see the light! I placed each light in its designated room and asked the electrician to get to work while I unpacked and placed other items.

When I walked into the boy's room, the wind was really taken out of my sails (pun intended). The light looked exactly like the picture, but it was a fraction of the size. I immediately checked the listing for the light and looked at the picture again. It looked huge in the picture. I scrolled down the listing and saw the measurements. There it was, mocking me: The diameter was twelve inches and that included the spikes that made it look like a compass. The fixture itself was probably closer to eight inches, making it one of the smallest overhead lights I have ever seen in my life.

I cringe as I tell this story. Of course, the designer should look carefully at every dimension before ordering things! In life, though, whether you're working on one room or a whole house, there are so many details that it's inevitable you'll miss something. That is one of the reasons I wrote this book: To give you a simple way to avoid the pitfalls I have discovered over the years. If you still find yourself in a pitfall, give yourself some grace.

Lighting Size

The most important aspect of a light fixture is not actually how it looks, but the size. The explosion of home decor on social media and the internet has been great for design, but it makes selection more challenging, as the images will likely be superimposed on backgrounds that aren't to scale or even real, so the item may appear to be different than the actual product.

Use this chart as your guide for selecting a chandelier or flush- or semiflush-mounted fixture based on size by width. Most websites will allow you to shop by size to narrow your search. If you're hanging a chandelier over a small area like a reading nook or piano, use the small room guideline for that area regardless of your overall room size.

Room size	Chandelier size (in inches)	Flush-mount and semiflush-mount size (in inches)
For large rooms (>250 sq. ft.)	No smaller than 36 wide and as large as 60 wide	No smaller than 22 wide and as large as 36 wide
For medium rooms (> 180 sq. ft.)	No smaller than 24 wide and as large as 48 wide	No smaller than 18 wide and as large as 30 wide
For small rooms (< 180 sq. ft.)	No smaller than 18 wide and as large as 30 wide	No smaller than 16 wide and as large as 24 wide

Placement

Each type of light fixture has its own placement guideline:

For a chandelier, the bottom of the fixture should hang as close to 7 ft. from the ground as possible. Use height to balance your space; if the ceilings are high and wide open, choose something more wide than it is tall. If your ceilings angle in and create a smaller opening, focus on fixtures that are taller but on the smaller side of the width guideline.

For a flush-mount or semiflush-mount, the bottom of the fixture should clear at least 6 ft. and 5 in. from the ground, and ideally 7 ft. If there are doors near the fixture make sure these can open and close without touching the fixture.

Lighting Needs

Some fixtures will give off enough light for an entire room, while others just add ambiance. Because your room probably has or will have recessed lighting, the actual amount of light from the fixture probably won't be a priority for you. If you do need the light to be bright, though, you'll want to focus on fixtures with more bulbs and fewer things to diffuse that light, like shades.

Style

After eliminating fixtures that are not the correct size and that won't provide the lighting you need, it will be easier to focus on the style you like. This comes down to personal taste, of course, but I am offering a few simple style recommendations to help guide your choice.

Hanging Fixtures

Traditional bulb chandeliers are what most people picture when thinking of a chandelier, with arms that come from the center and support candle-like bulbs. Think *Beauty and the Beast*. It's a classic look and does not need to be elaborate. If you're unsure of style, opt for a chandelier with fewer flourishes and cleaner lines.

Shade chandeliers are typical bulb chandeliers with individual shades. Shade chandeliers provide a cozy feeling and are especially good for living rooms with high ceilings because they add warmth. Shades also create an opportunity to add something trendy without committing to the look because the shades can always be removed or replaced. Scalloped shades, woven shades, and the empire (tapered) style are currently gaining popularity.

Sputnik chandeliers and globe fixtures have a super modern appeal and can add a cool element to most spaces. If your design feels too simple, infusing the room with this style of fixture will give you a huge design payoff.

Semiflush chandeliers are smaller fixtures that are hung close to the ceiling, but not flush with it. They provide the glamor of a chandelier in a smaller space. Crystal styles can add some formality, while lantern styles feel more casual.

Flush-mounted drum fixtures are large shades in the shape of a drum. These lights are great for rooms with lower ceilings. They provide warmth in a classic yet modern package.

Tiered flush-mounted lights are a ceiling-mounted style with graduated tiers to create an elegant look. They can give you the look of a chandelier even if you have standard height or low ceilings.

Sunburst-style flush-mounted lights mount to the ceiling and have decorative spikes coming out from the center. This style adds a chic element and is a good choice for rooms with lower ceilings.

Bowl ceiling fixtures (also known as "boob lights"—a term I believe I coined) are not recommended no matter how appealing the price. They read as builders' grade (think generic, inexpensive) and have little appeal.

> **Note about using rectangular or linear chandeliers:**
>
> A rectangular or linear chandelier is a fixture with the lights in a row, rather than having a round or square orientation. While I never say never in design, very few living spaces could benefit from this style. Rectangular or linear chandeliers look best over dining tables.

Sconces

Choose the size of your sconce(s) based on where they will be mounted. If a pair of sconces is being installed above a fireplace or a piece of furniture, they will likely flank a TV or picture frame. Use the TV or frame as an anchor, regardless of ceiling height. Start by looking at the height of the TV or frame. The midpoint of the sconce should be directly in the middle of the anchor.

Note that the midpoint of the sconce refers to the decorative fixture itself, not the backplate. The backplate is the piece that attaches to the wall and covers the power source. The location of the backplate is dependent on the style you choose. Using the midpoint of the fixture (not the backplate) is a good reference for the general placement of any style, and the electrician can determine the backplate location from there.

If you're flanking something with sconces, you want the height of the sconces themselves to be between 25 and 75 percent of the height of the item they're flanking. For example, if you are putting sconces on either side of a 36-inch square piece of art, the sconces should be between 9 and 27 inches tall.

If your sconces are being mounted on a wall without anything to anchor them, place them at a 60-inch height from the floor. Some sconces call for a slightly higher or lower placement because of the way they look, but 60 inches is a good starting point that will work for the majority of fixtures.

When choosing light fixtures for a wall, many sizes will work, but stay away from anything that seems small (don't go under 6 inches). Look at molding or door openings and give yourself at least 4 to 6 inches of space between molding or a door opening to install a sconce.

Sconces come in many different styles.

Candelabra sconces are exactly what they sound like—fixtures that somewhat resemble candles and come with either shades or bare bulbs. This look comes in a variety of styles, from modern to traditional. If you want this look but aren't sure whether to go with a shade, purchase one with clean lines and a shade because you can always remove it!

Pocket sconces and cylinder sconces are usually rounded and mount to the wall, covering the bulb. They have a more modern look that is only recently gaining popularity (again). If you like this style, they are a fun way to add some cutting-edge flair to your room. Don't invest too much in these fixtures though, because this trend may fade again.

Swing arm sconces have parts that are intended to be movable. I don't recommend swing arm sconces in your living area unless used for a reading nook. They're great next to a bed, but they never truly look polished in a decorative placement.

> **Note about candle sconces:**
>
> Please note that candelabra sconces are sometimes called candle sconces. However, a candle sconce usually refers to something mounted to a wall that is meant to hold an actual candle, not something electrified. Make sure to read the product description so you know what to expect when it arrives!
>
> If you opted not to install electrified sconces, candle sconces can add a beautiful element. Electrified sconces are always a better choice functionally, but candle sconces do provide an interesting alternative. If you would like a candle sconce, look for one with modern lines because these tend to lean toward ornate and old-fashioned looking.

Picture Frame Lights

Sizing picture frame lights is easy because many widths are compatible with many different sizes of picture frames. If you have a large single piece of art, then picture frame lights measuring 12 to 24 inches will work well. For a gallery wall, consider how many lights you plan to use and assess the size from there. I recommend one every 24 to 48 inches, depending on the size of the light. On a gallery wall that is 48 inches wide, you could use two small lights, perhaps around 8 inches each, or one large 24-inch light for the entire space.

You won't find much variation in the style of picture frame lights, and ultimately, it comes down to finish and detail. Barn-style sconces, which have large domes that cast light down, are sometimes used as picture frame lights, and I find they work well. You'll typically need more of these lights for a large gallery wall as they're not available in bigger widths like picture frame lights.

Go with your gut and don't overthink this one! They are meant to enhance the art, not be the star.

> **Note about battery-operated fixtures:**
>
> I love the idea of battery-operated lights, but I recommend you opt for wired fixtures instead. There are some decent-looking battery-operated picture frame lights, wall sconces, and even lamps, but the technology is evolving, and as of this writing, they are simply not robust enough to function well. My experience is that money spent on battery-operated fixtures is wasted—they don't provide adequate light and replacing the batteries starts as a nuisance and ultimately results in functionless lights. If wiring for sconces is out of the question, the battery-operated fixtures are certainly worth considering, but if you have the ability to wire, do that first.

Ceiling Fans

If you *must* have a ceiling fan, make it a good one. Opt for a larger-size fan: While a 42-inch fan is probably sufficient for a small- to medium-sized room, I don't recommend anything smaller than 52 inches. If your room is very large, consider two matching fans to cover the space.

Industrial styles tend to work best for fans. If that style does not work for your space, look for a fan that incorporates a unique fiber, like bamboo, for a distinctive look. You may need to shell out a little more cash to get a stylish fan, but I assure you this is not the place to skimp.

> **Amy's Favorites**
>
> I love so many light fixtures that it is hard to narrow down my favorites! Here are a few of my suggestions for each category:
>
> Chandelier: A Sputnik style but with a classic feature, like round bulbs
>
> Flush mount: A large drum shade fixture because it warms the space but is short enough for nearly any ceiling height.
>
> Picture frame light: A classic bar-style picture frame light. Visual Comfort & Co. has the best options, in my opinion.
>
> Sconce: A pair of candelabra sconces with beautiful shades, customized to coordinate with the room.
>
> Ceiling Fan: A simple fan with a sleek look, like the Monte Carlo Maverick, which only has three blades and can be ordered in a variety of finishes.

Once you've selected your light fixtures, confirm the date of your party and make sure you've left time for the electrician to install them.

With that confirmed, it is time to move from ceilings and walls to the floor.

Chapter 8 To-Do List

- Using your electrical plan, focus on one type of fixture for your room.
- Determine the best size range for the type of fixture you've selected.
- Determine how much light you need in your room.
- Find several fixture styles that would suit your room.
- Narrow your choices to three options.
- Print out images and hold them up to the mood board.
- Select your favorite.
- Repeat for the remaining fixture types.
- Purchase materials, including fixtures, dimmer switches and correct light bulbs.
- Confirm your party or gathering date.

Chapter 9

Rugs

At this point, you have completed the most difficult design elements. You took the time to analyze your space, carefully map the layout, and thoughtfully select the primary furniture. Now you get to make the room come alive! Which rug you choose has a big impact on your design.

An area rug always looks best in the living room. If you have wall-to-wall carpet or other flooring you do not like, replace it with hardwood or something similar. The visual payoff is always worth it. If adding hardwood is out of the question, that's okay, skip to the section about choosing your rug pattern and color.

> **Note about wall-to-wall carpeting:**
>
> It is worth noting that as of this writing the trade publication Business of Home reports that wall-to-wall carpeting is coming back in style. Personally, I have yet to see its appeal in a living room. Wall-to-wall carpet works nicely in a bedroom and occasionally in a

> self-contained living area. If you can avoid it in a space that flows from room to room, though, I suggest you do. While design is constantly changing, many general concepts (e.g., using hardwood in a living space) have true endurance. I would be shocked if in twenty years people are covering their hardwoods with wall-to-wall carpet.

Rug Size

Rooms look best with a rug that covers the majority of the floor. You may have beautiful flooring that you do not want to cover, but the rug will actually enhance your flooring. Using your floor plan, determine the largest-size rug that fits comfortably in the space. The standard area rug sizes, measured in feet, are as follows:

- 4 by 6
- 5 by 7
- 6 by 9
- 8 by 10
- 9 by 12
- 10 by 14
- 12 by 15

If your room is very long, has multiple seating areas, or is L-shaped, it may make sense to have two rugs. On your floor plan, start by drawing one rug around the main furniture grouping, with the edges about 6 inches from the wall. Ideally, all the legs of your furniture will sit on the rug. If a second rug makes sense for your space, draw that one too. Make sure your drawing allows floor vents to be uncovered.

Look at the size of the rectangle you drew. If one of the standard sizes is somewhat close to the dimensions you drew, you're in luck! You will be able to find a huge variety of colors and patterns in premade area rugs. The most fruitful selection will be in the smaller sizes, and you will find fewer options as you get to the 12 by 15-foot range.

If you have an area rug in mind, but it isn't available in the ideal size, you can still make it work. Look at the biggest size area rug that is available and fits in your space. Can you place it in a way that the front legs of your furniture all sit on it? That is the minimum requirement.

If the front legs of all your furniture sit on the rug and it does not feel proportionally small in the space, that may be all you need. If your heart is set on a rug that still feels small, layering rugs is an option for you. Using a tufted rug on top of a thinner natural weave rug is a beautiful way to utilize a smaller carpet that you like while still covering the space needed to make the room feel polished. Jute, seagrass, and similar neutral texture rugs are widely available both in ready-made or cut-to-order sizes, and they're usually quite affordable.

> **Note about area rug sizing:**
>
> Do not trust the size category that a rug is listed under online. For example, manufacturers will list a rug as being in the 8-by-10-foot category, but the rug may actually be 7 feet, 6 inches by 9 feet, 6 inches. I'm not sure how this became acceptable, but it is a common

> practice. As you narrow your search, make sure you put the exact size of the rug you're considering in your floor plan so you know what you will get.

If your desired size is not close to any of those standard sizes, you have alternate choices. Broadloom carpet is an excellent option for custom-sized rugs at a variety of price points. Broadloom is a category of carpet that comes from a large roll and is used for wall-to-wall carpeting. You may be picturing a slightly shaggy, mushroom-colored carpet from yesteryear, but you'll be pleased to learn that carpet stores carry options in a multitude of fibers and textures.

Once you have an approximate size in mind, measure the rug in the actual space to confirm there are no obstructions you have not considered.

Carpet Composition and Weave

When the concept of the washable rug was first introduced, I immediately ordered one for the area that leads to our pool. I was thinking of all the dirty, wet little feet that go in and out of there all summer long.

I knew it wouldn't feel like a real rug, but I was surprised when it came with the design printed on it. The texture is more like a fabric than a weave and the design is not woven through. This is not a problem for my pool entrance, but I do not think I would like it in my living room.

It has been four-and-a-half years since I received that rug, and a lot has happened. We got a puppy and have two children, so many bodily fluids have found their way on to that rug. In that time, though, I have never washed it. We have a washer and dryer no more than fifteen feet from the rug, so it is not an issue of convenience. Had this been my living room rug, I highly doubt I would have ever gone to the trouble of moving the furniture in order to wash it.

My takeaway is that the idea of washing your rug is fantastic, except for one small detail: you probably won't.

There are many new direct-to-consumer rug brands available, and a lot of them have excellent offerings. Make sure you know what you're getting before you order by understanding the fibers used to make your rug. It makes a difference in the look, feel, and durability. There are many choices, but the most common fibers that work well in a family or living room are as follows:

Wool rugs generally feel and look the best. Wool is the most trusted fiber and, in many ways, the most durable. It is generally more expensive than synthetic fibers but will hold up much longer. If you stain a wool rug, it is more likely to come out because the material is a natural fiber.

Polypropylene is the most common synthetic rug fiber, and because it's made from a plastic, it is stain resistant. The material does not feel as plush as wool. The fibers compress over time, but rugs made with polypropylene are very affordable so they tend to get replaced regularly.

Cotton, Silk, and Viscose make interesting rug fibers, but I do not recommend them for high-traffic areas because they are not very durable. Cotton rugs are affordable but feel like fabric and do not clean up very well. Silk and Viscose rugs are gorgeous, but the fibers are delicate and not conducive in most living areas.

How the rug is woven also plays a role in how it looks, feels, and performs. Most rugs are made with the following weaves:

Tufted rugs are the most common and are made by punching fibers into a backing material. This type of rug will shed when it is new, but the shedding typically dissipates after being vacuumed a few times. Inexpensive tufted wool rugs have a reputation for excessive shedding, though.

Hooked rugs are like tufted rugs, but instead of the yarns sticking straight up, they get woven into the backing. This type of rug is a favorite of mine because it looks great and is much more affordable than tufted rugs. A hooked rug rarely sheds.

Dhurrie-style rugs are flat-woven, almost like a thick fabric. The texture is not soft, but it is usually affordable and available in many great patterns. Dhurrie-style rugs do not shed.

Style Selection

At this point in the design, you've determined your color palette and the general style of your room. That will make it much easier to shop. As you look at different options, look at your favorites next to your mood board to ensure a cohesive look. Consider these three style categories:

Rugs with large patterns are great to integrate into a design with mostly neutral selections. If you lean toward solid fabric for furniture, consider letting the rug break the mold. A classic Persian style rug in a fresh color palette can work in nearly any space or a rug with an abstract modern design can make your room feel more luxe.

Striped, geometric, or tonal-patterned rugs allow you to develop your design without distracting too much from what you already have. Stripes and plaids are especially useful in designs that include florals or other organic patterns because they provide a counterbalance to all that whimsy.

Neutral rugs can be your best friend, especially if you have already made statements with your star and other items in the room. A classic textured ivory Berber looks great in nearly every space and can add brightness in a room that doesn't have much natural light.

> **Note about viewing rugs online:**
>
> The aerial view in which a rug is shown online is not representative of how it will look in your space, so keep this in mind when browsing. Some companies have alternate images of the rug in a room, which is helpful. As you look at the images, remind yourself which parts of the rug will be most visible and from what angle you will most commonly look at it.

> **Amy's favorites**
>
> If a room calls for a preppy patterned rug, I love using one of the brightly colored options from The Loom and Company. When I am looking for something modern, I search selections on Jaipur Living. Ernesta is a web based store that carries many beautiful neutral broadloom styles, and offers samples, too.

You have many options to select from and you're practiced when it comes to decision-making and placing orders, so pull the trigger and let's keep moving

Chapter 9 To-Do List

- Determine the size or range of sizes that best fit your room.
- Use your floor plan to understand what size rug is needed under your seating area.
- Measure the space in person to confirm there are no obstructions (e.g., vents).
- Browse rugs.
- Look at area rugs if a standard size works for you.
- Search broadloom options for a custom-sized rug.
- Place your order.

Chapter 10

Walls

It's finally here, the chapter many have been waiting for: How to pick a paint color. My advice? Don't paint! Just kidding. Perhaps you should paint your living room. Before you do, though, please consider the design-boosting alternative: wallpaper.

Are you still reading? Not everyone likes wallpaper. When I first started my business very few people were interested in wallpaper, as a lot of homes had old, ugly wallpaper that was extremely difficult to remove. It was hard to get anyone to install it, but I persevered. Much to my delight, wallpaper went from being something I had to beg clients to consider to something they hired me specifically to select. Admittedly, you may not yet be in that camp, so let me make my plea. Wallpaper does not need to have a big pattern. My favorite wall covering option is a grass cloth, or sometimes a vinyl grass cloth imitation that is either neutral or a soft color. It adds texture and warmth to a room. It looks better than paint 100 percent of the time. And wallcovering may not be as expensive as you think. As they have soared in popularity, some prices have come down, and the availability has increased.

Many wall treatments are significantly more durable than paint. A vinyl wallcovering is one of the most enduring things I can put in a family room, and as my client's children do their worst, my clients thank me for it.

> **Note about peel-and-stick wallpaper:**
>
> Peel and stick is really popular at the moment, but I recommend you stay away from it for this room. I use it in kids' rooms because their tastes change with the seasons, but my experience is that using it in a family room is a waste of time. The material isn't necessarily less expensive, and while it may seem easier to hang, it is actually more difficult. If you want to hang wallpaper yourself, you'll have more luck watching a YouTube video and putting up the real thing. My professional installer won't hang peel and stick becase he says it is too hard to work with; he can't get a clean cut because the material stretches. If professionals find it difficult to install, you shouldn't be struggling with it in one of your main living spaces.

Types of Wallpaper

While you can choose from many materials to make wallcoverings, consider these three categories:

Traditional paper is printed with a pattern. It typically comes in rolls that are 27 inches wide. The patterns match from roll to roll so when you hang it, the seams will be almost imperceptible. Patterns work well in small spaces, like a nook, or on a single accent wall. You will also find some wallpapers that have a very small pattern or textured look, and these work well in place of wall paint.

Grass cloth is a broad term I am using for any wallcovering made of a natural texture. It is usually made in rolls that are 36 inches in width and the material is woven to create the effect. Due to the natural origin of grass cloth, there is no pattern to match. The seams will be visible when it is hung. The texture and seaming is considered to be a very sophisticated look.

Vinyl wallcovering is made with vinyl—a super durable material. It comes in a variety of patterns and colors. Many companies make vinyl that looks like grass cloth with a texture similar to the real thing.

If you chose wallpaper as the star for your room, this is the time to let it shine! Whether it is the star or just a pattern that appeals to you and works with your mood board, determine if your room would most benefit from the pattern in one area or on all of the walls.

If you like the idea of a wallcovering without a pattern, you can use it in the same way you would use paint. Light neutral colors always look excellent and texture makes them feel less bland. If you want to bring in a color, look at your mood board to see which ones will flow with your room. The color should appear somewhere else in the room, perhaps on a fabric or piece of art.

I don't recommend dark colors for your wallcoverings in the living room. I love the look of a moody space, but I typically reserve this for dining rooms and powder rooms. Unless your space is very large and filled with natural light, keep the color on the lighter side.

> **Note about measuring for wallpaper:**
>
> To decide how much paper you need, some math is required. If someone else is hanging the paper for you, always ask that person to tell you the number of rolls the job will require.
>
> If you are hanging the paper yourself, calculate the length and number of strips of paper needed to cover your space. Start with the height of your wall and add the dimension of one pattern repeat to make sure you have enough to move it up or down to match. From there, I find it easiest to walk around the room, measuring out each width of paper as you go. Once you know how many strips of paper you need, use the measurements of your paper to determine how many strips come in each double roll. From there, you can calculate how many rolls you need to get the number of strips necessary for your room. Wallpaper is typically

> packaged in double rolls but sold in single rolls. This means you will almost always need to buy increments of two.
>
> It does not hurt to have a professional installer give you a quote, even if you plan to hang the paper yourself. They may give you a price you can't refuse, or at the very least they can confirm the number of rolls you need to order.

Wall Paint

When I was renovating my living room in 2012, I asked the painter who painted my client's homes to do the job for me. I gave him the color and went to work. I wanted something bold in the space, so I was very excited to see it at the end of the day.

When I saw the color, I gasped, and not in a good way. It was just wrong. The color had mutated on my walls, and even with only the first coat applied, I knew I could not wait this one out. I had made a big mistake. Sure, this happens to people all the time, but choosing paint colors was my job!

I went to my painter with my tail between my legs and asked him to start over with a different color. "You can never, ever tell anyone about this," I said with distress. The new color went up and the room looked fantastic. I have never spoken of that day since, until now.

Picking a paint color is not easy for anyone, and apparently, that includes some people whose job it is to select it. I have learned a few tricks over the years to ensure a good selection.

Start with a color that appears elsewhere in the room. The color could be from a tiny design on a pillow you plan to use or it could be the color of the sofa. As long as it appears somewhere else, it will feel cohesive.

Always, always, always pick a color with a neutral undertone. The paint deck may look appealing with its rainbow of colors, but just because they exist does not mean they should be used. Most brands have a specific grouping of more muted colors, and that is where you want to look for anything that goes on the walls.

Consider the option one shade lighter than the color you like. When the paint goes on your walls in multiple coats, it will reflect onto itself, which will make it appear darker and more intense. Take the time to get a sample of the paint and put a 12-inch swatch on each wall. Look at the swatch morning, noon, and night to see what the lighting does to it.

As you look at your mood board and the items you have assembled thus far, decide whether a neutral or a color is right for your space. I find a light neutral gives me the ability to play around with pattern and color on accessories and accent furniture. If you want to make a statement with color, go with something ethereal and bright. Dark colors have a place in the home, but it is rarely in the living room.

Trim Paint

There are some really cool things you can do with trim paint, but in general trim looks best painted white. In more than 90 percent of rooms I recommend a white semigloss. As you may already know, there are hundreds of shades of white paint. But I have good news: They don't make that much of a difference!

I consider white paint to fall into one of two categories: bright white or ivory. For most rooms I recommend going the bright white route because this looks better and crisper in most spaces. If you want a more sophisticated look and have a nice amount of natural light, using a paint with an ivory tone will work well for you. Always use a semigloss finish for your trim.

> **Note about using color on your trim:**
>
> If you have lots of natural sunlight and large millwork or a feature wall that is adjacent to your trim, painting it a color could be an excellent choice for you. Use the rules we used for wall color: select something with a neutral undertone that appears elsewhere in the room.

Ceiling Paint

Much like my trim paint suggestion, for ceiling color I recommend a bright white, but one with a super flat (not satin, eggshell, or semigloss) finish in nearly all rooms. Occasionally I'll put wallpaper on a ceiling or use a gloss paint, but this is the exception and not the rule. Every ceiling in my own home is bright white. Ceilings are best painted white because it makes the space above feel light and airy.

If you're lucky enough to have a vaulted ceiling, the opportunities open up for you to play around. I still typically use a bright white in this situation, but I often add some millwork and sometimes a textured wallpaper. Paint itself does not make a ceiling feel special, but when combined with other details like deep crown molding or trim detail, you can create a really special look.

> ### Amy's Favorites
>
> Okay, Okay you want an actual paint color suggestion. I get it. The following Sherwin-Williams colors have never failed me:
>
> Agreeable Grey SW7029 (which is really more of a beige) for a neutral in rooms that have natural light
>
> Shoji White SW7042 for a neutral in rooms that don't have much natural light
>
> West Highland White SW7566 for trim, which gives you an elegant bright white
>
> Extra White SW7066 for ceilings
>
> Storm Cloud SW6249 to add color to built-in bookcases, interior doors, and similar features

Chapter 10 To-Do List

- Determine what type of wall covering is best for your room.
- Decide whether wall coverings will cover all walls or just an accent wall.
- Look at your mood board and choose a color that meshes with other items in the space.
- Choose a ceiling paint.
- Choose a trim paint.
- Purchase paint or wallpaper.
- Hire a painter or paper hanger, if needed.

Chapter 11

Accent Furniture

While you selected your primary seating and center table, you added a few accent furniture placeholders—a console table here, a side table there. At this point you will add dimension and personality to the room by selecting accent pieces that are cohesive with the space. If you've already spent a lot of your budget by this point, you're in luck, as accent furniture has many affordable options and designer tricks.

Side Tables

Side tables are an excellent way to bring in warmth if the room needs it. Wood tones are great for grounding a space, and you will find many options for tables in wood. Alternatively, if your primary selections feel heavy (perhaps you selected a dark sofa and wood coffee table), this is your chance to tweak the look to include some lighter items; opt for a table painted in a soft color or something made of acrylic or glass.

If you like the way it looks and it meshes with your other choices, it is the right choice! Trust yourself.

When picking a side table, pay special attention to the height of the table. Manufacturers often list a table as both a bedside table and a side table, even if the height is more suited for one or the other. The arms of your sofa, or lack thereof, will also affect the height of your side tables. Most sofas have an arm height of around 24 inches and look best with a 24-inch-tall table. Your table can be a few inches shorter than the arm, but it should not be taller. If one part of your sofa or sectional is armless, opt for a table that is about 20 inches tall, which is slightly taller than seat height but close enough not to pull the eye.

Consider the angle you'll be looking at this table from. If your furniture is anchored on a rug in the center of the room and not touching the wall, you want to make sure that your side tables look great from every direction. Some tables are not finished on the back, as the assumption is they'll be placed against the wall. Alternatively, sometimes side tables get tucked between a wall and a chair, and we barely see them at all. If your table will be tucked away, worry only about how the top looks—don't spend money on a beautiful piece that won't get any airtime.

Consider the footprint your side table takes up as well. C-shaped side tables are popular now and are great because the base can be tucked under a sofa. These tables are super functional, especially if you want to maximize the space around your sofa while still having a place to put things.

If space is an issue, and this can happen in even the most spacious rooms purely due to layout, a drink drop table—

big enough only for a drink—may do the trick. Drink drop tables can be as small as 5 inches in diameter and fit nearly anywhere.

Console Tables

Most rooms have a spot for a console table, which can be an incredible addition to your room. A console table adds elegance, a useful tabletop, and some storage space. It can also be one of the most affordable pieces to add to a room.

Console tables look best when they become part of a wall feature. Place it below a beautiful piece of art or gallery of photos. If you opt for something with a low shelf, add baskets for storage and warmth. If you choose a style that is open beneath, the space provides the perfect place to tuck ottomans for additional seating and beauty.

Photography by Bartholomew Studio
Art by Sharon Garlepp

Accent Chairs and Ottomans

Accent seating is one of the more fun parts of putting together a room because we can typically find something that is striking and reasonably priced. Decorative ottomans are some of the most useful pieces because they add comfort when placed in front of chairs but are also able to be relocated to inconspicuous spots.

Accent chairs are available in a wide range of colors and patterns. If you're able to buy a top-tier accent chair, you will appreciate the quality in the long run. But tier-three brands also carry some more affordable yet stylish accent chairs, so this is a good category in which to save money.

The most important consideration regarding accent furniture is whether you have a place for it. I know how tempting it is to bring home that fun chair you saw at HomeGoods, but if it does not have a home in your room, it will actually degrade your design. Look at where you plotted accent furniture way back in chapter 2, and feel free to make adjustments as long as everything has a home.

Most spaces will have two side tables and one console table. Yours may vary, and if you don't find perfect accent pieces while completing this chapter, you may find one when shopping for accessories (chapter 14).

Chapter 11 To-Do List

- Revisit the place-holders you made for accent furniture.
- Search for furniture—side tables, console tables, and accent chairs—to fit these spaces.
- Order accent furniture.

Chapter 12

Window Treatments

Few things enhance a room the way window treatments do. Every window looks best when it is dressed, but you need to determine whether that treatment serves a purpose or is just there to look pretty. If you need privacy or to filter the light in your room, you will want to choose a style that can be made with the function you need.

While you have loads of options, Roman shades and fan pleat draperies are two styles that have worked in 99 percent of the projects I've worked on and always look great.

Roman Shades

Roman shades are window coverings that can be pulled down for privacy, and when pulled up, make soft folds. This style offers a modern look that isn't too fussy but is classic enough for any style decor.

Roman shades are typically either made with fabric or are woven from a natural material like bamboo. I will refer to these options as fabric shades or woven shades.

Roman shades can be *inside mount* (inside the frame) or *outside mount* (mounted on the wall above the frame). I generally prefer an outside mount Roman shade because it looks more generous. Occasionally the molding around a window calls for an inside mount. If your window has a Craftsman-style casing (molding with a ledge on top) or a very deep sill, hanging it inside is probably best. If you don't feel strongly about it one way or another, choose the outside mount.

For either fabric or woven shades, you'll get the best result if you contact a local window treatment store and have a representative come to your house to measure and bring samples to see in your room. It is not the most affordable way to get window treatments, but it saves you a lot of work and guarantees a professional result. Using a company that carries Hunter Douglas or a similar brand will also give you the option for motorization—an upgrade worth every penny in my book.

As of this writing some new motorized shade brands have emerged, but my experimentation shows that those companies have not yet developed their technology enough to seamlessly integrate with existing smart home systems. I expect the technology to improve, but I am still wary of lesser-known electronic brands that may or may not be available in the future to replace or repair the product if need be.

If bringing in a window treatment company is not in the cards for you, you have plenty of other options. Ready-made woven shades are easy to find and can look nearly as good as custom shades. Choose ready-made woven shades based on the width of your window. Amazon carries many options and allows you to search by width. For inside mount shades, measure the width at the top, middle, and bottom of your window and choose the smallest dimension as the width to shop for. This ensures that the shade will fit even if the window isn't quite square. Shop for shades that are either the exact dimension of your window or as much as an inch narrower. For outside mount shades, measure the width of the outside molding and choose shades that are that dimension or up to an inch wider. In both cases the closer to the width dimension, the better. The length of the shades should be longer than the window itself. The shade folds into itself, so when the shade is down, any extra length adds nice folds at the bottom.

I do not recommend ordering fabric shades from a big website like Amazon, but you can get the same look without a big expense from other sources. Roman shades are relatively easy to make, which means you may be able to hire someone to make them for you. Etsy is a good resource for customized Roman shades, or they could be a project for a friendly relative or neighbor who has sewing experience. Don't make them yourself unless you're adept at sewing, but if you are, by all means go for it!

There are some mainstream brands that offer fabric Roman shades in a variety of sizes. I have used Pottery Barn shades, and while they may not look quite as nice as a custom shade, they're quite good. The convenience of a ready-made shade is valuable, and if that gets you closer to a finished space, it is well worth it.

Roman Shade Mechanism

Roman shades are made with a variety of different mechanisms for raising and lowering them. Whether you are custom ordering your shades or making them yourself, understanding the mechanism they use will make for a smooth installation.

A cord cleat system is the most affordable and easy to make. It is a simple string system in which you pull the string to pull up the shade and then wrap the string around a metal piece—the cleat—installed on the wall next to the window. For some projects, I prefer the cord cleat because of its simplicity. Nearly everyone understands how to use it, which you may be surprised to learn is not the case for other Roman shade mechanisms. One disadvantage is that the shades need to be "dressed" every time they go up and down, meaning you'll need to gently straighten the fabric so that it maintains its nice folds. It is a minor task but worth noting.

The cord lock system is the next step up, and you may recognize it from miniblinds of yesteryear. When you pull the cord it locks into place, and if you want to pull it down you need to angle the cord away from the shade while pulling to unlock the mechanism. This style inevitably gets locked in the wrong spot or someone tries to pull it down without understanding how to unlock it. I rarely use this type of mechanism, simply because other systems are less problematic over time.

The chain system, sometimes referred to by its brand name RollEase, is a nice system with a tube mechanism and a chain to roll the shade up and down. While it's a good choice and a mostly reliable system, it's typically only a few dollars less than a true cordless system, which is usually preferred.

A cordless system uses the same tube mechanism as the chain system, but without the chain. You pull it down to lock it in place, and a gentle tug releases the mechanism and allows you to raise it. This system, along with the chain system, doesn't malfunction nearly as often as the cord lock system, but due to its more intricate nature, a malfunction may require a trade professional to repair it. This is one of the downsides to this system.

Automatic system. The automatic system is the best option, and if it weren't so costly, I would have it installed in every room. The shades are operated by using a switch on the wall (and often with an additional remote control and the option to integrate the shades into a smart home system). You can set a schedule so either the shades go up or down at the same time every day or rise and fall with the sun. After years of pulling cords and dressing shades, I cannot express the joy the automated system gives me. We have it in our primary bedroom and I still smile every time it engages.

Drapes

A few years ago I was putting together a fabulous dining room for a client. We had already installed a gorgeous light fixture and grass cloth on the walls. The final element was to hang beautiful silk drapes with a chic ribbon trim. On installation day I gazed lovingly at my creation. Not to pat myself on the back, but this room looked incredible.

A moment later, the air conditioning kicked on. Suddenly one panel of the drapes was blown up like a balloon. What's worse is it started to move back and forth like one of those blow-up dancing guys you see outside a car wash. All the other panels hung patiently, as if embarrassed by the rogue panel.

I felt a pit in my stomach. How had I missed this? I had considered the floor vent when ordering the rug—I just hadn't realized it would affect the drapes.

I honestly did not know what to do. I'm used to thinking on my feet because there are many hiccups in the design process. This time, though, I was up against something that felt much more powerful than anything I've ever been up against before: forced air.

The client came into the room before I could gather my composure. He asked what we could do about the balloon drape. I laughed and asked, "Do you really need that vent?" He kind of chuckled and said, "Yes." He explained this was the only vent in the room and the wall of windows created a greenhouse effect, heating up the room midday. They depended on that vent to cool the room.

"If we could just direct the air . . . " I tapered off with no real solution. He said, "Oh, what about one of these?" He walked into his office and returned with a rounded plastic vent cover. He put it on the vent and the air now shot out parallel to the floor instead of perpendicular. The car wash guy settled and lined up with his fellow drapes. "They're actually great for airflow," he said.

This shows you have to consider so much beyond the elements used in the design. If you want one less decision, go with a fan pleat drape. I cut my teeth in design selling window treatments, and even though I've overseen the installation of hundreds of different styles, the fan pleat (sometimes called the euro pleat) drape remains king of my heart. It is a simple drape made by folding the material with four pleats every four inches. The fan pleat is tacked at the top and is cousin to the pinch pleat, which is tacked a few inches from the top. A good drape will have buckram (a thick webbed material used to help fabric hold its shape) at the top, a 4-inch double-turned hem at the bottom, and hidden weights in the corners. A well-made drape is a beautiful thing.

If custom-made drapes are in your budget or on the edge of your budget, indulge. They are worth every penny. If you opt for custom-made drapes, you can skip to the fabric selection section. If custom-made drapes are not in your budget, read on.

To order ready-made drapes, search based on the overall length you need. You can calculate this by first deciding where the rod will be mounted. In most cases, the rod will be above the window frame, a minimum of four inches above the molding. If you can hang your drapes even higher, that is great! Longer drapes accentuate ceiling height. Using the measurement from the expected rod placement to the floor, determine which general length from the available options is closest. The increments in which they are available are typically 84 inches, 96 inches, 104 inches, and 120 inches. The drape can be slightly longer than your measurement, but it should not be shorter. If you plan to open and close these drapes on a regular basis, look at the width of the window and determine how many panels are necessary to cover the space. This will vary according to fabric and manufacturer.

Decorative drapes can be achieved with just one panel hanging on either side of a standard size window. If your widow is wider than 48 inches, use multiple panels to get a fuller look.

If you plan to open and close the drapes, you will most likely need multiple panels to ensure they're wide enough. Multiply the width of the window by 1.5 to get the width necessary to adequately cover the windows.

Ordering a pleated drapery style from a website like Ballard Designs, Pottery Barn, or Restoration Hardware will generally give you a decent result. Avoid alterations to ready made drapes to keep the cost down. At this price point additional expenses may put you in a situation where you are better off ordering custom drapes.

If you are working with a tight budget, it's possible to achieve a stylish look using affordable, ready-made drapes and making a few tweaks. Hang these drapes on fabulous hardware and add a nice, thick trim to the edges to achieve a professional look. I've ordered drapes that cost 29 dollars per panel from Amazon, added trim for about the same cost, and was able to get a nice look for the window for less than 150 dollars. Keep in mind someone has to attach the trim, which can be done with a glue gun. The trim is a key element because it enhances the look and covers the ends where there may be imperfect seams.

Sourcing trim can be as simple as picking a ribbon that appeals to you or as elaborate as ordering from a luxury brand like my favorite, Samuel & Sons. If you are selecting a ribbon, choose one that is thick enough so you can't see where it attaches with hot glue. A satin ribbon is too thin, but a grosgrain or woven ribbon works beautifully.

I do not recommend buying semicustom drapes. You'll get the right size but end up paying nearly as much as for custom drapes without any guarantee about the construction or fabric quality. My opinion is that for draperies you should either save a lot or splurge on something good; nothing in between.

Choosing Fabric for Drapes or Roman Shades

If you order from a window treatment store, you likely will have a selection of fabrics to choose from, and you may be able to supply your own fabric as well. You'll have similar options if you buy something from a store on Etsy. Ready-made brands will give you fewer options, but they're generally good choices.

Either way, selecting your own fabric can be overwhelming because there are so many great options! The design world has changed *drastically* since I began my business in 2010, and you will find an incredible number of resources. You not only have access to the high-end fabrics that used to be exclusive to designers, but you can also use on-demand printing companies that allow you to choose from a plethora of options. I love Spoonflower.com for truly unique patterns.

When ordering fabric online, use the rules below to make sure you get what you're expecting:

Scale. Make sure you understand the scale of the pattern, that is how many times the pattern will show up on your drape or shade.

Material (also known as ground). Know which kind of material the design will be printed on, and if possible, request a sample of it.

Color. Request a sample of the color because screens do not always give an accurate depiction of color.

Statement or Background?

Look at your mood board and the other elements you have already selected or want to see in your room. Use this information to determine how window treatments will help balance your design. For example, if a bold-patterned wallpaper is on your list, I recommend that you go with solid drapes or shades.

If you are leaning toward mostly neutrals in your space— perhaps a beige sofa and light wall color— window treatments are an opportunity to infuse some personality. A large floral drape can absolutely make a space, and if you don't have much else going, do it! The pattern doesn't need to be floral, of course, a geometric or other patterns can make a statement too. Choose what speaks to you.

Pattern Scale

The most important consideration when selecting a pattern for shades or drapes is considering the scale. For shades, you will only see a portion of that fabric, but you will see it flat and face-to-face. On drapes, you will see a much larger stretch of fabric, but the pattern will be muffled in the folds of the fabric. For this reason, stripes and plaids that work well on Roman shades don't always translate on drapes. If you want to use a stripe, go for something tone on tone (little contrast in the colors) so your eye does not get confused looking for the stripe to repeat regularly.

I find drape fabrics work best in either large-scale or small-scale patterns. A big repeat (the measurement of how large the fabric design is before it appears again) is great on drapes. A dainty dot or flower works well too, as long as it blends together in a way that makes it feel almost neutral. If you like a geometric pattern as this designer does, go for something that has at least a medium repeat in scale. This typically falls in the 12-inch-repeat range or larger. Anything smaller can, as my mother would say, make your eyes jump.

> **Amy's Favorites**
>
> I love to use patterns, but I often opt for a solid fabric for window treatments because it makes it easy to mix in with other fabrics. One way to make solid fabric feel more luxe is to add a beautiful trim to the edge of the shade or drape. Whether it is a tape, braid, or tassel, this is a great way to customize the drapes and help them coordinate with other elements in the room.

Privacy and Light Filtering

You have a few different privacy options for your shade or drapes. Use the table below to determine what is most useful for you.

Need	Best solution
Privacy during the day	Light-filtering lining: provides privacy without making your space dark
Reduce glare on TV	Standard lining: stops the glare but does not darken your space as much as blackout lining does
Privacy only at night	Standard lining or blackout lining: either provides complete privacy
Reduce greenhouse effect when not using the space during the day	Blackout lining: keeps out heat

Hardware

Pleated drapes require sturdy hardware to hold up all that beautiful fabric:

The rod is the pole upon which drapes hang. It should be about 20 inches longer than the width of the window itself, to allow the drape to hang beyond the glass of the window. Standard rods are ideal but may need to be cut down to size. Telescoping rods will fit a variety of lengths. They are less sturdy but still do the trick.

Brackets are installed on the wall and support the rod. Install a bracket for every 48 inches of rod that is being supported.

Rings are used to attach each pleat with a *drapery hook*, a small metalic piece that resembles a paperclip but has pointed ends. Do not attach your drapes with clips. If your hardware comes with clips, remove them and replace them with drapery hooks.

Finials or end caps go on the end of the rod to give it a polished look.

Rod sets are useful, but you may need to order multiple sets to meet your needs. Look at the number of pleats in your drapes to determine how many rings are needed and look at the length of the rod to figure out how many brackets you'll need.

If you're hanging a rod over a window that is more than 8 feet wide, you can join multiple smaller rods with a splice. Make sure you place a bracket at the joint to cover it.

Installation

When I am still getting to know a client I offer many different options to gauge their level of involvement and also their budget. Some clients want my help selecting draperies but are willing to hang them to save the money on professional installation. Many clients think they want to hang their own drapes to save money but in the end ask me to bring in an installer because, well, life.

On one occasion I asked a new client if she or her husband would like to hire a professional to install the drapes and told her the cost, which at that time was $250. Her response was, "Yes, because that's cheaper than a divorce." I laughed and continue to use this as my follow-up statement each time I offer professional installation.

Styles come and go in design, but as far as I can tell this advice never has: Hang your drapes high and wide to get the best look. The rod can hang above your window, at least 4 inches above (space permitting) and even higher if desired. The rod should be wider than the window molding: Add about 20 inches to the window measurement to allow 10 inches on either side for the drape to stack. This maximizes the glass that shows when the drapes are open, which looks great and keeps your room bright.

The installation of your window treatments will bring you a sense that the room is nearly complete, and the next steps will be the icing on that cake.

Chapter 12 To-Do List

- Decide which type of window treatment you plan to use.

For Roman shades:

- Choose fabric or woven shades.
- Measure the window.
- Order shades.
- Hire an installer or install them yourself.

For draperies:

- Choose ready- or custom-made drapes. Determine the length you need.
- If using ready-made drapes, determine the length you need.
- Choose fabric for the drapes.
- Order drapes.
- Consider whether you will add trim to ready-made drapes.
- Select hardware.
- Hire an installer or install them yourself.

Chapter 13

Wall Art

Every wall in your living room is an opportunity to make a statement, but that doesn't mean you have to hang art on every wall. The space you leave blank is just as important as the space you cover. It's a choice either way.

Choose Your Leading Wall

Look around your space because each wall presents a different opportunity. Start by choosing your leading wall, typically the wall with the most amount of wall space or the area that is begging to display something: Perhaps it is an empty space above a fireplace or the sofa, or a wall above a console table that looks empty.

With the lead wall in mind, determine how much of it should be covered in art. The exact amount will vary, but for the most part I recommend you fill roughly 70 percent of the empty space. For example, if the space over a fireplace is 8 feet wide, the frames should span about 67 inches. The actual dimension can be adjusted slightly depending on what you put there. One bold art piece could fill less space, perhaps even 48 inches, but no less because you should not stray too far from the target. A collection of framed photos could exceed that 67 inches and get closer to 84 inches. The idea is to create an imaginary box to fill, which will prevent you from ending up with two small pieces of art in a space that should have a large installation.

Use the options below to address your leading wall.

Photography

Photos are a great way to personalize the space and are fitting in a living area. The trick is to hang photos intentionally. Whether you want to hang a photo of your family, your guitar, or your dog, map it out carefully to make sure it is done artistically and fits with the other items in the space.

Choose photos that feature the things you love, favoring shots that are more natural and less posed. For a large wall, mix in some landscapes or pictures of meaningful objects to create a beautiful collection that feels elevated.

In order to achieve a high-end, polished look, use large black-and-white photos printed with a matte finish. Photos in this application look best when they are large, so have them printed at 11 by 14 inches or bigger.

Look for large frames with large mats, ideally 4 inches wide or more. Frames with premade mats make it easy and often provide the best result. Consider these photo arrangements:

Diptych or triptych is the fancy word for a grouping of two or three things meant to be hung together. The frames in this application should be the same finish, but they do not need to be the same size or orientation. It looks best when the frames are close in size, however. In order to execute this look, align your frames vertically or horizontally depending on the space. There should be about 2 inches of space between the frames.

A gallery wall makes family photos look artistic, takes minimal effort and is relatively inexpensive. Choose frames that are the same size and finish, and hang them in a grid pattern. This looks especially good with a picture frame sconce over the gallery, and it creates a fantastic night light with ambiance. Use the target dimension you calculated to fill the leading wall to determine how many frames will work best in your space.

A photo wall collection is similar to a gallery wall but looks more comfortable and curated. Gather a collection of frames that are cohesive in some way but are of varying sizes. All of the frames should be 8 by 10 inches or larger. Using the target dimension you calculated for the primary wall, lay out your frames on the ground, about 2 inches apart. Arrange them so that larger frames are spread out from each other and the orientation of the frames is varied throughout. Ideally, this will form a rectangle overall, but it will not be perfect. Use the layout on the ground as your guide to hang the photos on the wall.

Amy's Favorites

There are many great resources for frames, but my favorite is the Icon collection from Crate & Barrel. The frames are made from black-painted wood and the collection offers a variety of sizes, including a 24-inch square with a mat opening that is 11 inches square. Not all frames of this size come with real glass, but this one does.

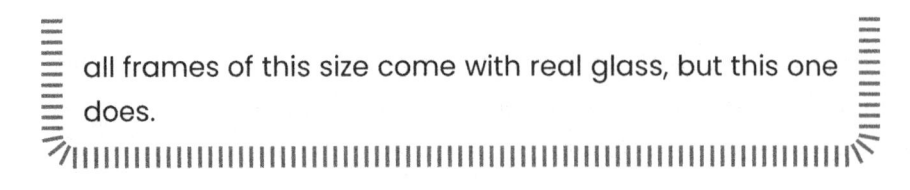

Art

If you already have a truly special piece of art, display it! Notice I said *truly special*? Do not hang something for the sake of having something there. If you have art that is valuable but you don't enjoy looking at it every day, then it has no value to you.

If you have art you love, make it a prominent feature in the room. If it is not already the size needed to properly address your primary space, add complementary pieces to fill out the space. Look for pieces with some of the same colors, and utilize frames that coordinate to make your art installation feel cohesive.

If you do not have art but want a unique piece, you can achieve that in many ways! Consider working with a gallery or art consultant who will help you select something that is not only beautiful in the space, but is also an investment.

If a gallery or art consultant is not in your budget at the moment, that is not a problem. With the addition of websites like Minted.com, art has become accessible in recent years. Many of the products on these sites are customizable and can be framed before they arrive at your home. These sites generally offer art prints, which are perfectly fine to use in your space. If you want something that shows brushstrokes and texture, though, you'll likely need to seek out another resource.

Local artists are a great resource for original art that doesn't break the budget. There is something chic about utilizing local artists too. Many artists will take on commissions, meaning you ask the artist to create something using a concept or colors you like.

Etsy.com offers a robust supply of art options, including prints and files you can print yourself. When you print your own, the quality is sometimes compromised, so select a file that is meant to be printed in the scale you need to get a beautiful piece of art for a reasonable price. To increase the quality, consider having it printed at a local print shop, a FedEx store, or through an online service. Some websites will print your art and also frame it for a reasonable price—bonus!

Art by Andrea Moran

Framing Your Art

There are many great ways to frame your art. When it comes to reframing a piece you already have, going to a local frame store is always the best option. The professionals there will walk you through the process, help you select mats and frames, and assemble it all for you.

If you're on a budget, you can frame things yourself. First, determine what type of frame you need. If your art is on a stretched canvas it will need a different type of frame than something that hangs behind glass. I find that canvas looks best with a floating frame, which is a thin frame that attaches to the back of the art and reveals a small gap between the art and the frame. It's easy to order floating frames online and assemble them yourself.

> **Note about framing canvases:**
>
> People ask me if their art on canvas really needs a frame. The answer is always yes! It's an easy upgrade for any piece of art. Bare canvases feel unpolished, but when framed they look upscale.

If your art is on paper and needs to go behind glass, there are a couple of ways to tackle it. If you have an original piece, some companies allow you to mail the art to them and will return it to you professionally framed. Depending on your choices, however, it can be pricey. Another disadvantage is that you may not be able to see the actual frame in person.

If you would like to frame art yourself, the key is choosing the right sized frame and mat. As with photos, choosing a frame that comes with a mat is your best bet. If you can find one with a larger mat or a mat with texture, you get bonus points! If you cannot locate a frame that suits your space and comes with a mat, you can order these items separately. As long as they're compatible, it will look great. Pay special attention to sizing, because mats have two different dimensions, one for the overall size and a second for the mat opening. For example, an 11-by-14-inch mat may have an 8-by-10-inch opening. In this scenario your piece of art should be 8 by 10 inches and your frame 11 by 14 inches. It sounds quite obvious as I type it, but I know from experience how easy it is to confuse these measurements!

> **Note about other types of wall hangings:**
> There are other things you can hang on your walls besides photos and art, and some of them are very cool. Overall, though, and for the purpose of keeping this look achievable, I don't recommend them. Wall sculptures, tapestries, and word art should be used sparingly. The exceptions to this rule would be anything that is precious or reflective of your family or culture and that also fits with the space. If you possess something like that, treat it just like an art piece. If not, stay out of that section of HomeGoods and the internet.

Adorn Your Other Walls

The suggestions made for your leading wall can apply to the other walls in your space as well. Working clockwise from the leading wall, look at each space and ask, "Is there a spot that feels blank?" If you aren't sure, the answer is no. Your instinct may be to hang something in every space but resist that urge. Leaving a space empty is sometimes the best way to enhance the room! Not only does the brain like to have visual spots to rest, fewer frames make the other wall hangings more important.

If your room has more than one large wall that is empty, treat this other wall differently than the leading wall. If you opted for a photo gallery on the leading wall, this one should get one or two large pieces of art. Likewise, if you went for a large piece of art on your lead wall, this wall should get a few smaller pieces, possibly photos. Unlike the leading wall, you do not need to fill 70 percent of this space, but you do need to make your wall hangings feel proportional. There is no rule for gauging what will look proportionate, but use a target of 50 percent as your guide.

As you look at the additional walls, consider if a small area could benefit from smaller frames. A space between windows or near an entry is usually a good choice for this. Using the concept of a diptych or triptych, choose smaller frames for this area.

Hanging Your Art

When hanging art, start with the midpoint of the art piece at about 60 inches from the floor. It is common for people to hang art too high, but it should really be at eye level. Use your piece as a guide: If it feels too low and bottom heavy, move it up an inch; if it starts to feel like it is floating, move it down an inch or two. Use your judgment and trust your gut, no matter what the other people in your space have to say. There is a tendency to overanalyze things when they are first installed, but after living with it for a day or two, it feels completely natural.

Your room is likely looking great by now, and you can use this time to tweak anything you like. Look around at all of the beautiful things that have come together, and if there is any color, shape, or pattern you'd still like to see in your space, insert it during the accessory phase, which I will cover in the next chapter.

Chapter 13 To-Do List

- Choose your leading wall.
- Determine the target dimension to cover.
- Choose between photography or art.
- Choose frames that work with your design and frame the art or photos.
- Look at the remaining walls and determine which could benefit from wall hangings.
- Choose wall hangings.
- Hang wall art and photos.

Chapter 14

Accessories

I worked with a lovely client who had an impressive collection of artifacts her parents had acquired while traveling the world. This left my client with an incredible collection of items, many of which were valuable. Even though her home was large, she had not figured out how to display the items and they ended up crowded on shelves.

The pieces were remarkable but were not necessarily what I would typically use to accessorize a room. It was a traditional home and these global accents had a completely different vibe. I knew that in order to make sense of it all, I would need to find commonalities in the artifacts and create a feature wall. I sorted through the items and began to pull things from different areas of the home.

Many of the items were carved wood, and the existing bookcase was also wood, so I added some grass cloth to the back of the shelves to make sure the wood objects would not blend in. What came together was a visually stunning compilation that became the star of the room.

When the client came in to see the finished project, she was moved to tears. She said she felt her parents' sense of adventure was finally being honored in her home. That made me cry too!

A truly curated space will include accessories that are meaningful to you and the people you love. The objects must be cohesive with the room, of course. For example. my son loves turtles, so when I came across a brass paperweight in the shape of a turtle, I bought it without question. As you shop, look for items that inspire you.

Objets d'Art

Objets d'art is a fancy way to say doodads, and however insignificant they may seem, they actually play an important role in creating a polished space. Sculptural pieces add life to a room by adding color, infusing humor, or displaying something meaningful to you.

Base Accessories

Your thingamajigs can be anything and everything as long as they are cohesive to the room design. To achieve cohesiveness, start with a few similar, larger items. One of the easiest and best-looking ways to achieve this look is to purchase multiple pieces of pottery in the same finish. I am partial to white—there is something so striking about all-white pottery, especially if set against a background with a color or texture. If your room is full of solids, you may choose something with a pattern, like blue and white pottery or a collection of vases with stripes.

Glass items are readily available in various colors or can be painted to work with your decor. Look for a few antique glass items in one color on Etsy, eBay, or in thrift stores. Another way to get this look is to gather a varied collection of clear glass vases and swirl the insides with some paint in your preferred accent color.

Whatever your collection is, this will be the base for your accessory design. The size of your collection will vary depending on where you plan to display your accessories. Use these guidelines for the number of base accessories I recommend for various spaces:

- Room with a large bookcase or similar display: ten to fourteen pieces
- Room with a bookcase or display: six to eight pieces
- Room without bookcase or display: two to three pieces

Other Sculptural Items

This base allows you to add a few other personal accessories and still have consistency. Look for objects that represent something meaningful to you, or simply look around your home for the small things that make you smile. These can be metal or wood or can incorporate a color that appears on your mood board.

I had a lot of fun working with a client who wanted everything to be just right. She was interested in making every space beautiful, and as you know by now, that's kinda my jam. She was willing to start over on everything—if what she owned wasn't a match for her gorgeous new space, good riddance!

She did not feel sentimental about getting rid of things if they did not jibe.

We had painted her beautiful built-ins a bright red; a risky move for sure, but she trusted me on it. I knew the red would not only bring in the color the open floor plan called for, but because the big statement had already been made with color, I would be able to display a more eclectic group of accessories and include things she already owned.

As we went through her things, I admired one gorgeous piece after the other. That was, until I pulled out a strange-looking crocheted doll, about 4 inches tall, holding a pipe cleaner meant to look like a tennis racket. The doll had curly hair and wore a white shirt and purple shorts. It was unlike anything else in her entire house. I asked her what it was, and as she spoke, I saw her face light up. "My aunt made that for me when I was in high school," she said with a poignant smile. "I'll put it somewhere else." "No!" I said as I cradled it close to my body, "Anything that gets a reaction like that must be on display."

Among all of the pretty frames, pottery, and books, I found a perfect ledge for this little crochet doll. Because

the bookcase was so beautifully pulled together, the one oddity added just the right amount of warmth and humor to the space. I still smile when I look at that little doll, and I know my client does too.

If you have a snow globe, a mug made by a child, or another quirky little piece that is special to you, don't miss the opportunity to put it somewhere that makes you smile every day.

> **Note about mixing metals in your space:**
>
> You do not need to commit to one metal finish in your home or even in a room! Mixing gold, silver, bronze, and black is an upscale technique and gives the room texture. However, allow only one finish to take the lead, and bring in accents of other metals that fit the room stylistically. If the other items are different both in finish and style, they could disrupt the flow and draw the eye from your star.

Books

Books are my favorite thing to decorate with because they give me so many options! Big, thick coffee table books can incorporate colors I'd like to add or highlight in a space, and the topics can be selected to reflect the people who occupy the space. By stacking or standing books I can add height in certain places or width in others. I can even amplify small knickknacks by giving them a pedestal made of books.

Purchasing nice coffee table books is a great investment and they make great, albeit partially selfish, gifts for someone else who lives in your home. In my home we have loads of books about golf, most of which have never been read but that my husband still enjoys receiving on birthdays and holidays.

You can order books in certain colors to match your decor if you like, but a collection that is genuinely your own will be beautiful, no matter the colors. You'll be automatically drawn to covers that appeal to you, and you can always search for more in a certain color to enhance your room. There is no correct number of books to acquire for a space, but here are some guidelines:

- Room with a large bookcase or display area: twenty-five or more
- Room with a small bookcase or display area: twelve or more
- Room with no bookcase or display: three or more

Gather your books and look for insights on placement at the end of the chapter.

Picture Frames

It is nice to display photos of loved ones on shelves and walls, and the frames can add to your design as well. Metallic frames add a pop to a space, and wood frames can ground a room. Colored picture frames can integrate more of your accent color if the room needs it.

Keep your frame style fairly consistent. I have worked with clients who have many lovely frames of different styles, but when displayed in one space, they look like a mishmash. To avoid this, choose frames with the same finish, even if they have different designs. Arranging these will be easier if you purchase them in pairs: two of each style and two of each size.

Frames of varied sizes made with consistent frame materials create a collection, similar to an accessory base or gallery wall. As with books, there is no correct amount of frames to display, but the following guidelines generally work for most rooms:

- Room with a large built-in: twelve large frames, eight medium frames, five small frames, and at least two unique frames.
- Room with a small built-in or nook: six large frames, six medium frames, four small frames, and at least one unique frame.
- Room with no built-in: two large frames, four medium frames, two small frames, and at least one unique frame.

Frame size dimensions	
Frame size	Frame dimensions (in inches)
Large frames	12 by 16 or 11 by 14 mat with an 8 by 10 opening
Medium frames	8 by 10 mat with a 5 by 7 opening
Small frames	5 by 7 mat with a 4 by 6 opening or 4 by 6 frames with no mat
Unique frames	Small square or round frames, among other shapes

Plants

Adding plants to your space will add texture and beauty. The green of plants is a neutral that looks great in every room. Some clients want oodles of plants, but as the number of plants multiplies, the focus is taken away from the design and is directed toward the burgeoning greenhouse. For this reason I recommend you stick to one or two large plants per room and three or fewer small to medium plants.

To determine which plants to buy, consider their placement and not just what appeals to you. You may love a fiddle-leaf fig (who doesn't?), but if the only spot that works with the decor is a dark corner, neither you nor the plant will be happy in the long run. Look around your room and determine where the plant will look good and will also have enough sun to stay alive.

A plant in a beautiful stand looks great in front of a window (assuming there is ample space) and a small pot on a console adds just the right amount of green. Keep in mind that in addition to water and light, plants sometimes need other things, like trimming and repotting. If you don't mind handling that, great! If you have a black thumb, look at alternatives. Few things are uglier than a dead plant. I have a love/hate relationship with faux plants and have experimented over the years to find the right balance.

Faux succulents and boxwoods may be the easiest to work with. Many of the faux boxwood are real plants that have been preserved, and the natural element shows. Succulents can look remarkably real (or is it that even real succulents sometimes look fake?) and add the color and texture you're looking for.

Faux trees may be an excellent addition to your decor. This is not the spot to count your pennies, though. Invest in a good, realistic-looking tree to get the look.

Faux flowers are more difficult to incorporate because, I'll just say it, they look cheap. I have had the most success with faux flowers that are obviously faux, like those made of paper or metal. This style gives the look of flowers without trying to be actual flowers. Some of the best faux flowers I have purchased came from Anthropologie's garden store, Terrain.

> **Amy's Favorites**
>
> A pair of large plants or trees work well in many rooms, especially in a space behind a sofa that is otherwise not used. They are cheaper than adding more furniture and add a large-scale look to the room.
>
> If you do not have space for plants, stick with a few small succulents on a bookcase, windowsill, or center table. Trader Joe's offers some great potted plants that can last a remarkably long time, sometimes even without much sun.

Areas to Arrange

Your room will have several areas that look great with a few accessories, but don't be afraid to leave some spaces blank, too. As we discussed with wall art, an empty space is as much of a statement as those with decor. Bookcases, tabletops, and windowsills will be enhanced with a few accessories. Determine which areas in your space need some love and what already looks great as is.

Arranging Items on a Center Table

You can arrange accessories on a coffee table in many ways, but the easiest way to get a polished look is to put them on a decorative tray. Look for a tray that is on the larger side—a 24-inch square or round tray is a good proportion for most tables.

The tray is a great way to add a decor element that your room could use, perhaps some color. It's easy to customize a tray, whether that means ordering it on Etsy in the color of your choice or spray painting one you picked up elsewhere.

A tray allows you to create a nice-looking arrangement. Sure, it'll need to be tidied up every so often, but for the most part, things will be contained.

Choose a few large coffee table books to create a stack on the tray. If your tray can accommodate two stacks of coffee table books, that works too. Next, add a decorative lidded box, bowl, or a smaller tray to contain remote controls or to collect other miscellaneous items. I know that a tray within a tray seems silly, but it contains chaos.

Coasters are another essential addition to most center tables, and they provide a unique way to infuse color, humor, or personality into your space. Look for something that is visually cohesive with the room, but feel free to use word art or shapes here to give it a personal touch.

With the essential elements in place, choose one or two decorative pieces you'd like to add. I have a marble tic-tac-toe board that gets a surprising amount of use on my coffee table. A candle can be a nice addition here too. When you get flowers, replace one of these decorative items with the flowers until they no longer look fresh.

Arranging Items on Side Tables

Every side table will be different, but there are a few things that always work. If the back of the side table is against the wall, capitalize on this and use it to display some picture frames. Group picture frames with something decorative (like an object d'art) and leave the rest blank. If you occasionally pick up a little succulent or have a small vase of fresh flowers, add them here for a natural touch.

If your table is floating in the room, use decorative accessories without a back. Books and magazines are my first choice for tables like this, and I like it when guests actually pick up these items and thumb through them. Don't be afraid to put this book on display!

Arranging Items on a Window Sill, Console Table, or Similar Flat Surface

If you're lucky enough to have deep windowsills, use them to add some fun accessories that pull the space together. The same goes for console tables or other flat surfaces, and the overall size and number of items you display simply increases as the spaces get bigger. Each surface will get something from the base collection of accessories and a few additional items. The following table presents guidelines for each type of space:

Space size (in inches)	Largest item size (in inches)	Number of base accessories	Total number of accessories
Standard windowsill (about 36)	12–15	1–2	3–5
Medium console table (about 48)	15–18	2–3	4–6
Large table or credenza (about 72)	18–24	3–4	5–8

These surfaces look best when there is empty space in the middle of them. It's not the only way to do it, but it is usually the best way to do it. Put a large accessory on one side of the surface and another, slightly smaller accessory on the other. Step back and look at the balance. Does one side feel heavier than the other? If so, add an accessory to the lighter side, choosing one that complements the existing piece. Step back again. If you are working with a standard size windowsill, this may be all you need. In a larger area, see which side is lighter and add accordingly. Continue to do this until it feels complete, always leaving plenty of open space in the middle of your two groupings.

Arranging a Bookcase

Balance is key in every space, and this is especially true when placing items on bookshelves. Arrange your base accessories on the floor by size. As you look at each, which ones would pair nicely together? Perhaps there are two of a similar shape but different heights, or maybe a different pair that complements each other in some other way. If there are, group each pair as one piece.

Start with the two largest pieces, which will go in opposite corners of the bookshelf. Place the largest item on the top shelf of your bookcase and the second largest on the bottom shelf. It looks best if you put them in slightly different locations on their respective shelves. For example, the item on the top shelf could sit all the way on the left side and the item placed on the bottom shelf could go in the middle.

Repeat this step with the next two largest pieces, but this time fill two spots that balance what you have already placed. Using the example above, place the next largest accessory on the second shelf from the top, but this time on the right side. Place the next piece on the shelf above the bottom shelf, but this time all the way on the left. Assuming this is a classic five-shelf bookcase, put the next piece in the middle of the middle shelf.

Your placement will vary depending on the number of shelves you have, but the goal is to spread your base pieces out in a way that feels balanced but is not a mirror image. Move things around until you feel they are evenly spaced.

With these in place, you will add picture frames and plants, if applicable. Picture frames look best when grouped in pairs, usually with a taller frame slightly behind a smaller frame. Balance these in a similar way to the base accessories, using the open spaces as your guide for placement. Plants look great when grouped with a pair of frames or pottery, or you can use them to punctuate a book collection with something green.

You should still have some remaining space on your shelves, and this is where to place books. If you do not have space, take away a few pieces to see how it feels. The three main ways to add books with interest are as follows:

Use larger coffee table books as a platform for any small accessories or frames that feel dwarfed in the space. A stack of two or three books placed horizontally usually does the trick.

Use a row of books standing in height order from one side of the bookshelf. Place a heavy accessory or a bookend at the end of the row.

In the middle of an otherwise empty shelf, place a row of books in height order, this time ascending and then descending to fill the space. Add bookends to keep it looking polished.

Now that you've accessorized your space like a pro, it is time to show it off!

Chapter 14 To-Do List

- Select a group of base accessories and collect the amount that suits your room.
- Choose other sculptural accessories to incorporate.
- Gather the number of books needed for your space.
- Gather the number of picture frames desired for your room.
- Determine what type of plants will work in your space and purchase them.
- Arrange accessories in your room.

Chapter 15

Installation

With all of your selections in place, you can start putting together your living room in time for your party. Install or place your elements in this order:

1. Electrical
2. Construction such as drywall or woodwork, if applicable
3. Paint and wallcoverings
4. Rug
5. Furniture
6. Window treatments, art, and accessories

It is helpful to create a small window for the arrival and installation of your items. Get on your installer's schedule at least a few weeks in advance so their availability does not hold you back. Always leave a day or two in between contractors because there are inevitable delays and it is ideal to avoid overlap.

On nearly every job I have ever completed the client contacts me midway through installation with a concern. I can nearly predict the day I will get a call. It happens when some things have been put in the room, but we are still waiting on the rest.

It usually goes something like this: "I don't think the sofa is right. It looks huge in the space." Or "Would you please come take a look at this wallpaper? I think there is something wrong with the installation."

It is my job to talk them off the ledge and ask them to try not to overthink it until the room is fully put together. None of my clients have been dissatisfied with a room once all of the finishing touches were in place.

You have spent a lot of time, effort, and money on this room. When the elements of your room arrive one by one, you may begin to overanalyze them. Do your best to avoid this pitfall: Do not make any judgments until a *few days after* everything for the space has arrived. If you have any hesitation about your choices, you will be surprised to see how things come together when they're all in the space. Trust the process.

You may be thinking: "You're a professional, of course it looks good. What about us amateurs?" Give yourself some credit! You've gone through all the same steps as the professionals. You have visualized, measured, grouped ideas, made a mood board, and made wise choices. I can say with the utmost confidence that your room will come together beautifully.

When it does, enjoy your party and share your photos!

I am so incredibly grateful that you chose me to join you in this process. Pulling together a room is absolutely my favorite thing to do and walking you through the process has been an absolute pleasure. Leaving you here is bittersweet, but I hope to join you on another project soon.

Happy designing,

Amy Barrickman

PS Don't forget to rotate your cushions!

Acknowledgments:

I could not have written this book, or even become an interior designer without my husband and best friend, Bo. You supported me even when it was difficult to do so, and you continue to do so any time I come up with some new venture, no matter how off-the-wall it may seem.

Thank you to my sister, Sarah, who is the reason I was able to write this book. Without your encouragement and management of my social media, I would not have been able to achieve my goal.

Thank you to my wonderful daughter, Bryn, just for being you. You share my love of writing, and I know you'll have your own published work someday soon.

Thank you to my incredible son, Trip, for inspiring me everyday. I love you and can't wait to see what you do with your many talents!

Thank you to my father, Dave Deatrich, for teaching me how to sell and that everything is sales. Your example gave me the confidence to publish (and ultimately promote) a book.

Thank you to my mother, Leslie Deatrich, for being my biggest cheerleader and teaching me to take every idea to the next level.

Thank you to all of the incredible clients I have had along the way. Each and every one of you has taught me something, and I am grateful that you put your trust in me.

Thank you to Sharon, for being a great colleague and friend and providing your beautiful art to grace the pages of this book.

Thank you to Lindsay, who wasn't looking to help produce and promote a book, but did so anyway.

Thank you to my lifelong best friend Caroline, for your unadulterated support over the last three decades.

Thank you to all the family and friends who have given me support by telling people about the book, posting reviews, and purchasing it. I really appreciate all you have done to help me!

Thank you to Beacon Point LLC, who edited this book thoughtfully and protected my voice throughout the process.

Thank you to Erin at Beacon Point LLC who proofread this book.

Thank you to the team at SPS, for their beautiful cover and formatting work. I also thank them for supporting me as I took the process in my own direction.

Thank you to Allison Davis, who coached me through this journey and was just as excited as I was every step of the way.

Thank you to Chandler Bolt, who wrote a book that inspired me, and created the tools that helped me realize my lifelong dream of becoming a published author.

Your home is never finished.

Visit www.BarrickmanDesign.com for a growing assortment of resources, including these free instant downloads:

Living Room Measurement and Layout Guide

Helpful tools to help you plan your space, including graph paper, sample layouts, and to-scale furniture footprints to play around with in your room design.

Gallery Wall Tips & Tricks

A step-by-step guide to creating a beautiful feature in your home using photographs.

Follow me
@BarrickmanDesign
for regular design tips and updates!

Amy Leah Barrickman

Amy has always loved to write and studied journalism at the Pennsylvania State University. She owns the interior design firm Barrickman Design, located on the main line of Philadelphia, and she features easily digestible home design tips and tricks on her firm's social media accounts.

These short videos have not only caught the attention of many subscribers on TikTok, YouTube, Instagram, and FaceBook but also of QVC, where Amy now appears as an on-air design expert.

Amy is also a trained actress, having appeared in several feature-length and short films. She hopes to someday return to the stage to appear in musicals like she did in high school.

Amy lives outside of Philadelphia with her husband, their two children, and one five-pound dog. She loves spending time manicuring every inch of the 1940 home and property they acquired in 2018. She hopes not to finish this labor of love anytime soon, for then they will need to move.

Thank You For Reading This Book!

I would appreciate your feedback and help to make the next version of this book and future books better!

Would you please take two minutes now to leave a helpful review on Amazon letting me know what you thought of the book?

It would really help me out!

Thank you so much!

Amy Leah Barrickman

Made in the USA
Columbia, SC
24 February 2025